THE LITTLE MUSKETEER®

ALL IN ONE AND ONE IN ALL

REMINDER ORGANIZER TRACKER KEEPER

PASSWORD BOOK, ADDRESS BOOK, CRYPTO JOURNAL, NFT TRACKER, IMPORTANT DATE KEEPER, HOME, SCHOOL, WORK, & SOCIAL LIFE ORGANIZER.

PUT THE LITTLE MUSKETEER® TO WORK FOR YOU!

Welcome to The Little Musketeer™

Your all-in-one solution for organizing your life! With its sleek design and user-friendly features, The Little Musketeer is not just a password keeper; it's a powerful assistant that helps you stay on top of everything that matters.

What's Inside:

- *Password Book:* Safely store and organize all your passwords in one secure place.
- *Address Book:* Keep track of important contacts and addresses effortlessly.
- *Crypto Journal:* Record and monitor your cryptocurrency investments and transactions.
- *NFT Tracker:* Stay updated on your non-fungible token assets with ease.
- *Important Date Keeper:* Never miss an important event or deadline again.
- *Home, School, Work & Social Life Organizer:* Categorize and manage different aspects of your life with ease.

Put The Little Musketeer to Work for You!

SATORI PUBLISHING

BY INDIES. FOR INDIES.

ISBN: 978-1-7373455-7-2

THIS BELONGS TO:

____

IF FOUND PLEASE RETURN TO:

____

____

____

____

If not returned, this book will self destruct in 3... 2... 1...

P.S. To the Finders Keepers Loosers Weepers Thief who might try to hack my accounts: Everything in here is a lie designed to plant malware, spyware, viruses, plague, disease, & the black death in YOUR electronics.
Don't say you weren't warned.

THE LITTLE MUSKETEER®

Dear Safe Keeper,

Welcome to The Little Musketeer - your ultimate companion for organizing your digital life and keeping your most important information at your fingertips! We understand the frustration of forgetting passwords, searching for essential details, and the hassle of filling out applications.

With The Little Musketeer, those worries are a thing of the past. This all-in-one reminder, organizer, tracker keeper empowers you to take control of your data securely. Unlike digital solutions, your information is safe from security breaches and accidental losses.

Your Little Musketeer is much more than a password keeper. It's a powerful tool that safeguards:

- Website usernames and passwords
- Internet security, network, and Wi-Fi information
- Crypto wallet and NFT details
- Personal social media and digital presence
- Important dates, holidays, birthdays, anniversaries
- School life, from high school to internships
- Home life, including previous addresses and finances
- Work life, with your employment history
- Social life, featuring personal references and acquaintances

Once you experience the efficiency and convenience of The Little Musketeer, you'll wonder how you ever managed without it. We're confident you'll love it as much as we do!

If you have any feedback or improvement suggestions, please don't hesitate to reach out. Your satisfaction is our priority.

Thank you for choosing The Little Musketeer! We hope it brings you joy, organization, and peace of mind.

Wishing you a well-organized and secure life!

Stay Safe,
The Little Musketeer Team

UNDERSTANDING BYTES

Unit	Abbreviation	Storage
Bit	B	Binary Digit, Single 1 or O
Nibble	-	4 bits
Byte/Octet	B	8 bits
Kilobyte	KB	1024 bytes
Megabyte	MB	1024 KB
Gigabyte	GB	1024 MB
Terabyte	TB	1024 GB
Petabyte	PB	1024 TB
Exabyte	EB	1024 PB
Zettabyte	ZB	1024 EB
Yottabyte	YB	1024 ZB

YOUR VERY OWN DECODER RING

How can you ensure the confidentiality of your private information? There's a chance that this might end up in the wrong hands someday. So, how can you guarantee that if that does happen, your personal information and your entire life won't be completely compromised? The solution lies in creating your own system for encoding and decoding. It should be a system that you understand well and will never forget. It can be as straightforward or intricate as you prefer, but keep in mind that the purpose of this approach is to counteract your tendency to forget complex information over time. Therefore, it's recommended to keep it simple and personal.

To help you get started with forming your secret code, consider these ideas:
Using Favorite Numbers: If your favorite number is 3, for instance, you can substitute the letter 'e' in your passwords with the number 3. For example, turn "Ocean" into "Oc3an" or "Oc#an." You record Ocean in the journal.
Incorporating Favorite Colors: If your favorite color is Blue, include "Blue" in every password. For instance, transform "BOcean" into "BlueOcean."
Using Familiar Names: If you frequently use your grandmother's name, Joyce, in your passwords, adopt a similar pattern. Turn "HerBicycle!23" into "JoyceBicycle!23."
Utilizing Personal Desires: If you've always wanted to visit Paris, let that desire guide you. Transform "GOhere&-2#3" into "GOparis&-2#3."
Creating Your Own Approach: Feel free to invent your own technique or even combine a couple of the methods mentioned above.

Remember, it's vital that the system you create is easy for you to remember but challenging for others to guess. Consistency is key—stick to this system at all times. Even seemingly unimportant accounts could be the gateway to more significant ones if someone gains access.

PRO TIP: Before you start recording any data, thoroughly review all sections and pages of this journal. There's a wealth of information and designated spots to organize it. By noting down details like your bank's website, user ID, password, and where you store account information and customer service numbers, you'll save space in the alphabetical listing for other websites. This proactive approach will save you time and effort in the long run.

HOW TO USE YOUR ALL-IN-ONE ONE-IN-ALL REMINDER ORGANIZER TRACKER KEEPER

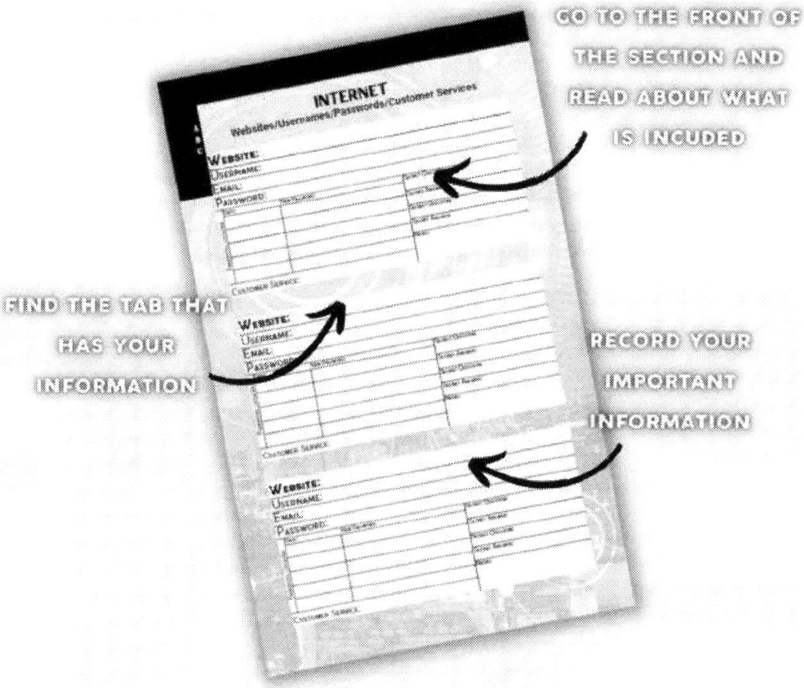

Important Legal Disclaimer Regarding the Use of this Journal

We advise against storing highly sensitive information in this journal, as it may be lost, stolen, or misplaced. Any information that you do decide to keep should be encoded to ensure that it remains secure and confidential. Please note that we cannot guarantee the safety of the information you choose to store in this journal, and we do not offer any implied warranties, promises, or obligations regarding its safety or secrecy.

INTERNET

Websites/Usernames/Passwords/Customer Services
Network Security/WiFi/Email Server/Software
Crypto Wallet/NFT Tracking
Social Media Accounts/ Digital Resume/Personal Websites

IMPORTANT DATES

Holidays
Birthdays
Anniversaries
Important Events

SCHOOL LIFE

Highschool
College
Graduate School
Internships
Associations

HOME LIFE

Places I've Lived/Neighbors
Personal Finances
Subscriptions
Mortgage/Insurance/Utilities/Inventory
Service Providers

WORK LIFE

Places I've Worked/Start & End/Address/Title
Organizations
Network

SOCIAL LIFE

Friends/References/Acquaintances
Social Clubs/Charities

THE INTERNET SECTION

Websites/Usernames/Passwords/Customer Services

Alphabetical listing of websites where you can store your usernames and passwords as well as customer service information, secret questions and answers as well as password updates with the date it changed.

Network Security/WiFi/Email Server/Software

From the provider, to the logistical information needed to access the servers, you user keys, license information and even reoccurring or renewal information. And of course, who to call when things go south.

Crypto Wallet/NFT Tracking

You can store your Crypto key, your wallet tracking and even your purchase and sales.

Social Media Accounts/ Digital Resume/Personal Websites

Store all of your social media account user ids and passwords as well as your personal digital footprint for easy access.

INTERNET

Websites/Usernames/Passwords/Customer Services
Network Security/WiFi/Email Server/Software
Crypto Wallet/NFT Tracking
Social Media Accounts/ Digital Resume/Personal Websites

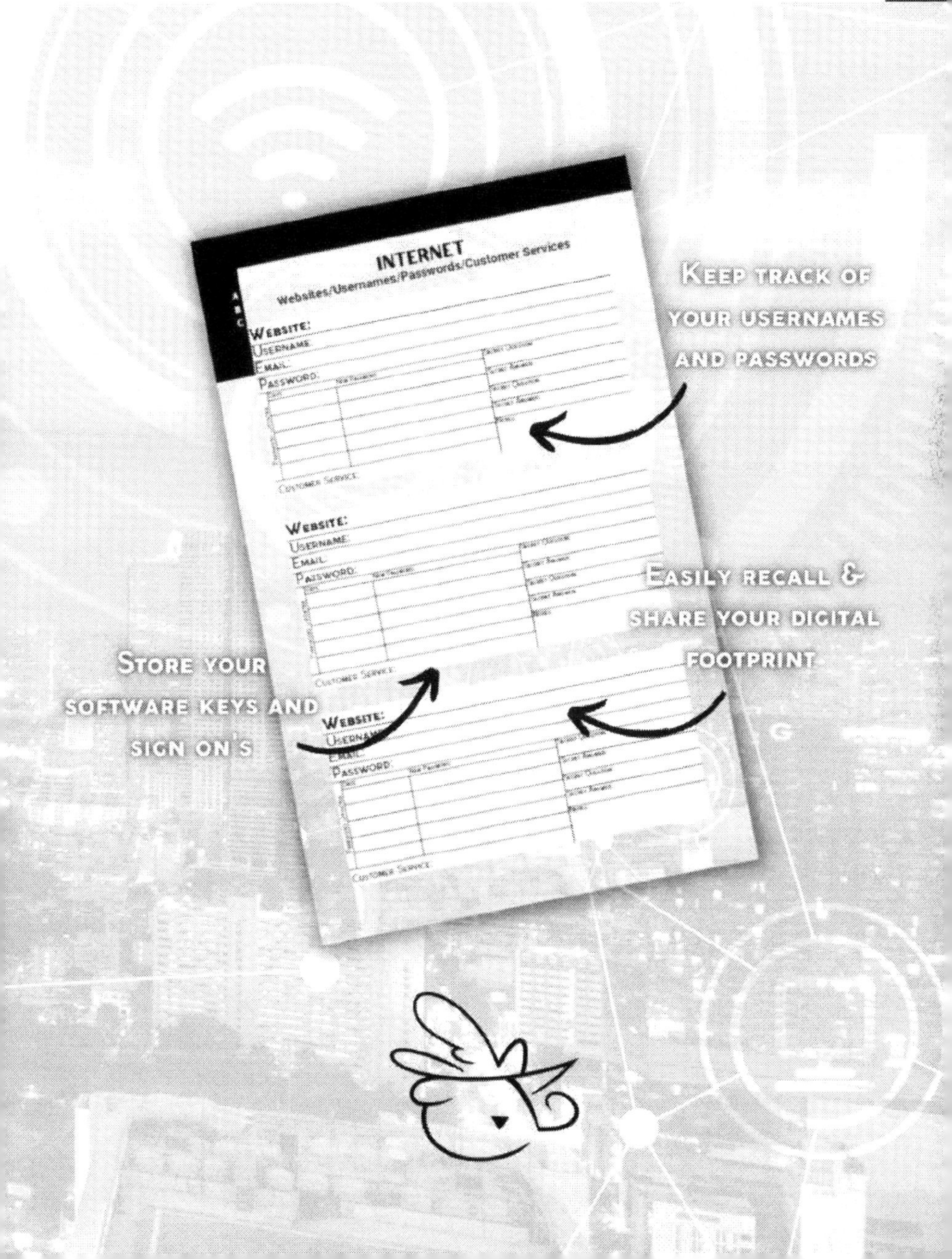

INTERNET

Websites/Usernames/Passwords/Customer Services

WEBSITE:

USERNAME:

EMAIL:

PASSWORD:

Password Updates: Date:	New Password:	Secret Question:
		Secret Answer:
		Secret Question:
		Secret Answer:
		Notes:

CUSTOMER SERVICE:

WEBSITE:

USERNAME:

EMAIL:

PASSWORD:

Password Updates: Date:	New Password:	Secret Question:
		Secret Answer:
		Secret Question:
		Secret Answer:
		Notes:

CUSTOMER SERVICE:

WEBSITE:

USERNAME:

EMAIL:

PASSWORD:

Password Updates: Date:	New Password:	Secret Question:
		Secret Answer:
		Secret Question:
		Secret Answer:
		Notes:

CUSTOMER SERVICE:

INTERNET

Websites/Usernames/Passwords/Customer Services

A
B
C

Website:

Username:

Email:

Password:

Password Updates: Date:	New Password:

Secret Question:

Secret Answer:

Secret Question:

Secret Answer:

Notes:

Customer Service:

Website:

Username:

Email:

Password:

Password Updates: Date:	New Password:

Secret Question:

Secret Answer:

Secret Question:

Secret Answer:

Notes:

Customer Service:

Website:

Username:

Email:

Password:

Password Updates: Date:	New Password:

Secret Question:

Secret Answer:

Secret Question:

Secret Answer:

Notes:

Customer Service:

INTERNET

Websites/Usernames/Passwords/Customer Services

Website:

Username:

Email:

Password:

Password Updates: Date:	New Password:	Secret Question:
		Secret Answer:
		Secret Question:
		Secret Answer:
		Notes:

Customer Service:

Website:

Username:

Email:

Password:

Password Updates: Date:	New Password:	Secret Question:
		Secret Answer:
		Secret Question:
		Secret Answer:
		Notes:

Customer Service:

Website:

Username:

Email:

Password:

Password Updates: Date:	New Password:	Secret Question:
		Secret Answer:
		Secret Question:
		Secret Answer:
		Notes:

Customer Service:

INTERNET

Websites/Usernames/Passwords/Customer Services

A
B
C

Website:

Username:

Email:

Password:

Password Updates: Date:	New Password:

Secret Question:

Secret Answer:

Secret Question:

Secret Answer:

Notes:

Customer Service:

Website:

Username:

Email:

Password:

Password Updates: Date:	New Password:

Secret Question:

Secret Answer:

Secret Question:

Secret Answer:

Notes:

Customer Service:

Website:

Username:

Email:

Password:

Password Updates: Date:	New Password:

Secret Question:

Secret Answer:

Secret Question:

Secret Answer:

Notes:

Customer Service:

INTERNET

Websites/Usernames/Passwords/Customer Services

WEBSITE:

USERNAME:

EMAIL:

PASSWORD:

PASSWORD UPDATES: DATE:	NEW PASSWORD:

SECRET QUESTION:

SECRET ANSWER:

SECRET QUESTION:

SECRET ANSWER:

NOTES:

CUSTOMER SERVICE:

WEBSITE:

USERNAME:

EMAIL:

PASSWORD:

PASSWORD UPDATES: DATE:	NEW PASSWORD:

SECRET QUESTION:

SECRET ANSWER:

SECRET QUESTION:

SECRET ANSWER:

NOTES:

CUSTOMER SERVICE:

WEBSITE:

USERNAME:

EMAIL:

PASSWORD:

PASSWORD UPDATES: DATE:	NEW PASSWORD:

SECRET QUESTION:

SECRET ANSWER:

SECRET QUESTION:

SECRET ANSWER:

NOTES:

CUSTOMER SERVICE:

INTERNET

Websites/Usernames/Passwords/Customer Services

Website:

Username:

Email:

Password:

Password Updates: Date:	New Password:

Secret Question:

Secret Answer:

Secret Question:

Secret Answer:

Notes:

Customer Service:

Website:

Username:

Email:

Password:

Password Updates: Date:	New Password:

Secret Question:

Secret Answer:

Secret Question:

Secret Answer:

Notes:

Customer Service:

Website:

Username:

Email:

Password:

Password Updates: Date:	New Password:

Secret Question:

Secret Answer:

Secret Question:

Secret Answer:

Notes:

Customer Service:

INTERNET

Websites/Usernames/Passwords/Customer Services

Website:

Username:

Email:

Password:

Date:	New Password:

Password Updates:

Secret Question:

Secret Answer:

Secret Question:

Secret Answer:

Notes:

Customer Service:

Website:

Username:

Email:

Password:

Date:	New Password:

Password Updates:

Secret Question:

Secret Answer:

Secret Question:

Secret Answer:

Notes:

Customer Service:

Website:

Username:

Email:

Password:

Date:	New Password:

Password Updates:

Secret Question:

Secret Answer:

Secret Question:

Secret Answer:

Notes:

Customer Service:

INTERNET

Websites/Usernames/Passwords/Customer Services

Website:

Username:

Email:

Password:

Password Updates: Date:	New Password:	Secret Question:
		Secret Answer:
		Secret Question:
		Secret Answer:
		Notes:

Customer Service:

Website:

Username:

Email:

Password:

Password Updates: Date:	New Password:	Secret Question:
		Secret Answer:
		Secret Question:
		Secret Answer:
		Notes:

Customer Service:

Website:

Username:

Email:

Password:

Password Updates: Date:	New Password:	Secret Question:
		Secret Answer:
		Secret Question:
		Secret Answer:
		Notes:

Customer Service:

INTERNET

Websites/Usernames/Passwords/Customer Services

Website:

Username:

Email:

Password:

Password Updates: Date:	New Password:

Secret Question:

Secret Answer:

Secret Question:

Secret Answer:

Notes:

Customer Service:

Website:

Username:

Email:

Password:

Password Updates: Date:	New Password:

Secret Question:

Secret Answer:

Secret Question:

Secret Answer:

Notes:

Customer Service:

Website:

Username:

Email:

Password:

Password Updates: Date:	New Password:

Secret Question:

Secret Answer:

Secret Question:

Secret Answer:

Notes:

Customer Service:

INTERNET

Websites/Usernames/Passwords/Customer Services

Website:

Username:

Email:

Password:

Password Updates:

Date:	New Password:

Secret Question:

Secret Answer:

Secret Question:

Secret Answer:

Notes:

Customer Service:

Website:

Username:

Email:

Password:

Password Updates:

Date:	New Password:

Secret Question:

Secret Answer:

Secret Question:

Secret Answer:

Notes:

Customer Service:

Website:

Username:

Email:

Password:

Password Updates:

Date:	New Password:

Secret Question:

Secret Answer:

Secret Question:

Secret Answer:

Notes:

Customer Service:

INTERNET

Websites/Usernames/Passwords/Customer Services

Website:

Username:

Email:

Password:

Password Updates: Date:	New Password:

Secret Question:

Secret Answer:

Secret Question:

Secret Answer:

Notes:

Customer Service:

Website:

Username:

Email:

Password:

Password Updates: Date:	New Password:

Secret Question:

Secret Answer:

Secret Question:

Secret Answer:

Notes:

Customer Service:

Website:

Username:

Email:

Password:

Password Updates: Date:	New Password:

Secret Question:

Secret Answer:

Secret Question:

Secret Answer:

Notes:

Customer Service:

INTERNET

Websites/Usernames/Passwords/Customer Services

Website:

Username:

Email:

Password:

Password Updates:

Date:	New Password:

Secret Question:

Secret Answer:

Secret Question:

Secret Answer:

Notes:

Customer Service:

Website:

Username:

Email:

Password:

Password Updates:

Date:	New Password:

Secret Question:

Secret Answer:

Secret Question:

Secret Answer:

Notes:

Customer Service:

Website:

Username:

Email:

Password:

Password Updates:

Date:	New Password:

Secret Question:

Secret Answer:

Secret Question:

Secret Answer:

Notes:

Customer Service:

INTERNET

Websites/Usernames/Passwords/Customer Services

Website:

Username:

Email:

Password:

Password Updates:

Date:	New Password:	
		Secret Question:
		Secret Answer:
		Secret Question:
		Secret Answer:
		Notes:

Customer Service:

Website:

Username:

Email:

Password:

Password Updates:

Date:	New Password:	
		Secret Question:
		Secret Answer:
		Secret Question:
		Secret Answer:
		Notes:

Customer Service:

Website:

Username:

Email:

Password:

Password Updates:

Date:	New Password:	
		Secret Question:
		Secret Answer:
		Secret Question:
		Secret Answer:
		Notes:

Customer Service:

INTERNET

Websites/Usernames/Passwords/Customer Services

WEBSITE:

USERNAME:

EMAIL:

PASSWORD:

PASSWORD UPDATES:

DATE:	NEW PASSWORD:

SECRET QUESTION:

SECRET ANSWER:

SECRET QUESTION:

SECRET ANSWER:

NOTES:

CUSTOMER SERVICE:

WEBSITE:

USERNAME:

EMAIL:

PASSWORD:

PASSWORD UPDATES:

DATE:	NEW PASSWORD:

SECRET QUESTION:

SECRET ANSWER:

SECRET QUESTION:

SECRET ANSWER:

NOTES:

CUSTOMER SERVICE:

WEBSITE:

USERNAME:

EMAIL:

PASSWORD:

PASSWORD UPDATES:

DATE:	NEW PASSWORD:

SECRET QUESTION:

SECRET ANSWER:

SECRET QUESTION:

SECRET ANSWER:

NOTES:

CUSTOMER SERVICE:

INTERNET

Websites/Usernames/Passwords/Customer Services

Website:

Username:

Email:

Password:

Password Updates:

Date:	New Password:

Secret Question:

Secret Answer:

Secret Question:

Secret Answer:

Notes:

Customer Service:

Website:

Username:

Email:

Password:

Password Updates:

Date:	New Password:

Secret Question:

Secret Answer:

Secret Question:

Secret Answer:

Notes:

Customer Service:

Website:

Username:

Email:

Password:

Password Updates:

Date:	New Password:

Secret Question:

Secret Answer:

Secret Question:

Secret Answer:

Notes:

Customer Service:

INTERNET

Websites/Usernames/Passwords/Customer Services

Website:

Username:

Email:

Password:

Date:	New Password:	
		Secret Question:
		Secret Answer:
		Secret Question:
		Secret Answer:
		Notes:

Password Updates:

Customer Service:

Website:

Username:

Email:

Password:

Date:	New Password:	
		Secret Question:
		Secret Answer:
		Secret Question:
		Secret Answer:
		Notes:

Password Updates:

Customer Service:

Website:

Username:

Email:

Password:

Date:	New Password:	
		Secret Question:
		Secret Answer:
		Secret Question:
		Secret Answer:
		Notes:

Password Updates:

Customer Service:

P
Q
R

INTERNET

Websites/Usernames/Passwords/Customer Services

Website:

Username:

Email:

Password:

Password Updates:

Date:	New Password:

Secret Question:

Secret Answer:

Secret Question:

Secret Answer:

Notes:

Customer Service:

Website:

Username:

Email:

Password:

Password Updates:

Date:	New Password:

Secret Question:

Secret Answer:

Secret Question:

Secret Answer:

Notes:

Customer Service:

Website:

Username:

Email:

Password:

Password Updates:

Date:	New Password:

Secret Question:

Secret Answer:

Secret Question:

Secret Answer:

Notes:

Customer Service:

INTERNET

Websites/Usernames/Passwords/Customer Services

Website:

Username:

Email:

Password:

Password Updates:

Date:	New Password:

Secret Question:

Secret Answer:

Secret Question:

Secret Answer:

Notes:

Customer Service:

Website:

Username:

Email:

Password:

Password Updates:

Date:	New Password:

Secret Question:

Secret Answer:

Secret Question:

Secret Answer:

Notes:

Customer Service:

Website:

Username:

Email:

Password:

Password Updates:

Date:	New Password:

Secret Question:

Secret Answer:

Secret Question:

Secret Answer:

Notes:

Customer Service:

INTERNET

Websites/Usernames/Passwords/Customer Services

Website:

Username:

Email:

Password:

Date:	New Password:	
		Secret Question:
		Secret Answer:
		Secret Question:
		Secret Answer:
		Notes:

Password Updates:

Customer Service:

Website:

Username:

Email:

Password:

Date:	New Password:	
		Secret Question:
		Secret Answer:
		Secret Question:
		Secret Answer:
		Notes:

Password Updates:

Customer Service:

Website:

Username:

Email:

Password:

Date:	New Password:	
		Secret Question:
		Secret Answer:
		Secret Question:
		Secret Answer:
		Notes:

Password Updates:

Customer Service:

INTERNET

Websites/Usernames/Passwords/Customer Services

Website:

Username:

Email:

Password:

Password Updates:

Date:	New Password:

Secret Question:

Secret Answer:

Secret Question:

Secret Answer:

Notes:

Customer Service:

Website:

Username:

Email:

Password:

Password Updates:

Date:	New Password:

Secret Question:

Secret Answer:

Secret Question:

Secret Answer:

Notes:

Customer Service:

Website:

Username:

Email:

Password:

Password Updates:

Date:	New Password:

Secret Question:

Secret Answer:

Secret Question:

Secret Answer:

Notes:

Customer Service:

INTERNET

Websites/Usernames/Passwords/Customer Services

Website:

Username:

Email:

Password:

Password Updates:

Date:	New Password:

Secret Question:

Secret Answer:

Secret Question:

Secret Answer:

Notes:

Customer Service:

Website:

Username:

Email:

Password:

Password Updates:

Date:	New Password:

Secret Question:

Secret Answer:

Secret Question:

Secret Answer:

Notes:

Customer Service:

Website:

Username:

Email:

Password:

Password Updates:

Date:	New Password:

Secret Question:

Secret Answer:

Secret Question:

Secret Answer:

Notes:

Customer Service:

INTERNET

Websites/Usernames/Passwords/Customer Services

Website:

Username:

Email:

Password:

Password Updates:

Date:	New Password:

Secret Question:

Secret Answer:

Secret Question:

Secret Answer:

Notes:

Customer Service:

Website:

Username:

Email:

Password:

Password Updates:

Date:	New Password:

Secret Question:

Secret Answer:

Secret Question:

Secret Answer:

Notes:

Customer Service:

Website:

Username:

Email:

Password:

Password Updates:

Date:	New Password:

Secret Question:

Secret Answer:

Secret Question:

Secret Answer:

Notes:

Customer Service:

V
W
X
Y
Z

INTERNET

Websites/Usernames/Passwords/Customer Services

WEBSITE:

USERNAME:

EMAIL:

PASSWORD:

PASSWORD UPDATES:

DATE:	NEW PASSWORD:	
		SECRET QUESTION:
		SECRET ANSWER:
		SECRET QUESTION:
		SECRET ANSWER:
		NOTES:

CUSTOMER SERVICE:

WEBSITE:

USERNAME:

EMAIL:

PASSWORD:

PASSWORD UPDATES:

DATE:	NEW PASSWORD:	
		SECRET QUESTION:
		SECRET ANSWER:
		SECRET QUESTION:
		SECRET ANSWER:
		NOTES:

CUSTOMER SERVICE:

WEBSITE:

USERNAME:

EMAIL:

PASSWORD:

PASSWORD UPDATES:

DATE:	NEW PASSWORD:	
		SECRET QUESTION:
		SECRET ANSWER:
		SECRET QUESTION:
		SECRET ANSWER:
		NOTES:

CUSTOMER SERVICE:

INTERNET

Websites/Usernames/Passwords/Customer Services

V
W
X
Y
Z

Website:

Username:

Email:

Password:

Password Updates: Date:	New Password:	
		Secret Question:
		Secret Answer:
		Secret Question:
		Secret Answer:
		Notes:

Customer Service:

Website:

Username:

Email:

Password:

Password Updates: Date:	New Password:	
		Secret Question:
		Secret Answer:
		Secret Question:
		Secret Answer:
		Notes:

Customer Service:

Website:

Username:

Email:

Password:

Password Updates: Date:	New Password:	
		Secret Question:
		Secret Answer:
		Secret Question:
		Secret Answer:
		Notes:

Customer Service:

INTERNET

Websites/Usernames/Passwords/Customer Services

Website:

Username:

Email:

Password:

Password Updates:

Date:	New Password:

Secret Question:

Secret Answer:

Secret Question:

Secret Answer:

Notes:

Customer Service:

Website:

Username:

Email:

Password:

Password Updates:

Date:	New Password:

Secret Question:

Secret Answer:

Secret Question:

Secret Answer:

Notes:

Customer Service:

Website:

Username:

Email:

Password:

Password Updates:

Date:	New Password:

Secret Question:

Secret Answer:

Secret Question:

Secret Answer:

Notes:

Customer Service:

INTERNET
Websites/Usernames/Passwords/Customer Services

V
W
X
Y
Z

WEBSITE:

USERNAME:

EMAIL:

PASSWORD:

PASSWORD UPDATES:

DATE:	NEW PASSWORD:

SECRET QUESTION:

SECRET ANSWER:

SECRET QUESTION:

SECRET ANSWER:

NOTES:

CUSTOMER SERVICE:

WEBSITE:

USERNAME:

EMAIL:

PASSWORD:

PASSWORD UPDATES:

DATE:	NEW PASSWORD:

SECRET QUESTION:

SECRET ANSWER:

SECRET QUESTION:

SECRET ANSWER:

NOTES:

CUSTOMER SERVICE:

WEBSITE:

USERNAME:

EMAIL:

PASSWORD:

PASSWORD UPDATES:

DATE:	NEW PASSWORD:

SECRET QUESTION:

SECRET ANSWER:

SECRET QUESTION:

SECRET ANSWER:

NOTES:

CUSTOMER SERVICE:

INTERNET

Websites/Usernames/Passwords/Customer Services

Website:

Username:

Email:

Password:

Password Updates:

Date:	New Password:

Secret Question:

Secret Answer:

Secret Question:

Secret Answer:

Notes:

Customer Service:

Website:

Username:

Email:

Password:

Password Updates:

Date:	New Password:

Secret Question:

Secret Answer:

Secret Question:

Secret Answer:

Notes:

Customer Service:

Website:

Username:

Email:

Password:

Password Updates:

Date:	New Password:

Secret Question:

Secret Answer:

Secret Question:

Secret Answer:

Notes:

Customer Service:

INTERNET

Network Security/WIFI/Email Server/Software

NETWORK

PROVIDER: **BROADBAND ID:**

USERNAME:

BACKUP EMAIL:

PASSWORD:

PASSWORD UPDATES: DATE:	NEW PASSWORD:	
		SECRET QUESTION:
		SECRET ANSWER:
		SECRET QUESTION:
		SECRET ANSWER:
		NOTES:

CUSTOMER SERVICE:

ADDITIONAL INFORMATION:

INTERNET

Network Security/WIFI/Email Server/Software

Provider: **Broadband ID:**

Username:

Backup Email:

Password:

Password Updates: Date:	New Password:

Secret Question:

Secret Answer:

Secret Question:

Secret Answer:

Notes:

Customer Service:

Additional Information:

INTERNET

Network Security/WIFI/Email Server/Software

NETWORK

Provider: **Broadband ID:**

Username:

Backup Email:

Password:

Password Updates:

Date:	New Password:

Secret Question:

Secret Answer:

Secret Question:

Secret Answer:

Notes:

Customer Service:

Additional Information:

INTERNET

Network Security/WIFI/Email Server/Software

Provider: **Broadband ID:**

Username:

Backup Email:

Password:

Password Updates:

Date:	New Password:

Secret Question:

Secret Answer:

Secret Question:

Secret Answer:

Notes:

Customer Service:

Additional Information:

INTERNET

Network Security/WIFI/Email Server/Software

BRAND: **MODEL:**

NETWORK NAME: NETWORK KEY:

ADMIN KEY: ADMIN URL:

USERNAME: PASSWORD:

PASSWORD UPDATES:

DATE:	NEW PASSWORD:

SECRET QUESTION:

SECRET ANSWER:

SECRET QUESTION:

SECRET ANSWER:

NOTES:

CUSTOMER SERVICE:

ADDITIONAL INFORMATION:

INTERNET

Network Security/WIFI/Email Server/Software

BRAND: **MODEL:**

NETWORK NAME: NETWORK KEY:

ADMIN KEY: ADMIN URL:

USERNAME: PASSWORD:

PASSWORD UPDATES:

DATE:	NEW PASSWORD:

SECRET QUESTION:

SECRET ANSWER:

SECRET QUESTION:

SECRET ANSWER:

NOTES:

CUSTOMER SERVICE:

ADDITIONAL INFORMATION:

INTERNET

Network Security/WIFI/Email Server/Software

Brand: | **Model:**

Network Name: | Network Key:

Admin Key: | Admin URL:

Username: | Password:

Password Updates:

Date:	New Password:

Secret Question:

Secret Answer:

Secret Question:

Secret Answer:

Notes:

Customer Service:

Additional Information:

W I F I

INTERNET

Network Security/WIFI/Email Server/Software

Brand: **Model:**

Network Name: Network Key:

Admin Key: Admin URL:

Username: Password:

Password Updates:

Date:	New Password:

Secret Question:

Secret Answer:

Secret Question:

Secret Answer:

Notes:

Customer Service:

Additional Information:

INTERNET

Network Security/WIFI/Email Server/Software

BRAND: **MODEL:**

NETWORK NAME: NETWORK KEY:

ADMIN KEY: ADMIN URL:

USERNAME: PASSWORD:

PASSWORD UPDATES:

DATE:	NEW PASSWORD:

SECRET QUESTION:

SECRET ANSWER:

SECRET QUESTION:

SECRET ANSWER:

NOTES:

CUSTOMER SERVICE:

ADDITIONAL INFORMATION:

W
I
F
I

INTERNET

Network Security/WIFI/Email Server/Software

BRAND: **MODEL:**

NETWORK NAME: NETWORK KEY:

ADMIN KEY: ADMIN URL:

USERNAME: PASSWORD:

PASSWORD UPDATES:

DATE:	NEW PASSWORD:

SECRET QUESTION:

SECRET ANSWER:

SECRET QUESTION:

SECRET ANSWER:

NOTES:

CUSTOMER SERVICE:

ADDITIONAL INFORMATION:

INTERNET

Network Security/WIFI/Email Server/Software

Email Provider: Outlook/Microsoft Office

Email Address: Name@outlook.com

IMAP Server: outlook.office365.com

IMAP Port: 993 Encryption Method: TLS

POP Server: outlook.office365.com

POP Port: 995 Encryption Method: TLS

SMTP Server: smtp-mail.outlook.com

SMTP Port: 587 Encryption Method: STARTTLS

Additional Information:

Email Provider: Outlook/Microsoft Office

Email Address: Name@outlook.com

IMAP Server: outlook.office365.com

IMAP Port: 993 Encryption Method: TLS

POP Server: outlook.office365.com

POP Port: 995 Encryption Method: TLS

SMTP Server: smtp-mail.outlook.com

SMTP Port: 587 Encryption Method: STARTTLS

Additional Information:

INTERNET

Network Security/WIFI/Email Server/Software

Email Provider: Outlook/Microsoft Office

Email Address: Name@outlook.com

IMAP Server: outlook.office365.com

IMAP Port: 993 Encryption Method: TLS

POP Server: outlook.office365.com

POP Port: 995 Encryption Method: TLS

SMTP Server: smtp-mail.outlook.com

SMTP Port: 587 Encryption Method: STARTTLS

Additional Information:

Email Provider: Outlook/Microsoft Office

Email Address: Name@outlook.com

IMAP Server: outlook.office365.com

IMAP Port: 993 Encryption Method: TLS

POP Server: outlook.office365.com

POP Port: 995 Encryption Method: TLS

SMTP Server: smtp-mail.outlook.com

SMTP Port: 587 Encryption Method: STARTTLS

Additional Information:

INTERNET

Network Security/WIFI/Email Server/Software

Email Provider: Outlook/Microsoft Office

Email Address: Name@outlook.com

IMAP Server: outlook.office365.com

IMAP Port: 993 Encryption Method: TLS

POP Server: outlook.office365.com

POP Port: 995 Encryption Method: TLS

SMTP Server: smtp-mail.outlook.com

SMTP Port: 587 Encryption Method: STARTTLS

Additional Information:

Email Provider: Outlook/Microsoft Office

Email Address: Name@outlook.com

IMAP Server: outlook.office365.com

IMAP Port: 993 Encryption Method: TLS

POP Server: outlook.office365.com

POP Port: 995 Encryption Method: TLS

SMTP Server: smtp-mail.outlook.com

SMTP Port: 587 Encryption Method: STARTTLS

Additional Information:

INTERNET

Network Security/WIFI/Email Server/Software

Email Provider: Outlook/Microsoft Office
Email Address: Name@outlook.com
IMAP Server: outlook.office365.com
IMAP Port: 993 Encryption Method: TLS
POP Server: outlook.office365.com
POP Port: 995 Encryption Method: TLS
SMTP Server: smtp-mail.outlook.com
SMTP Port: 587 Encryption Method: STARTTLS
Additional Information:

Email Provider: Outlook/Microsoft Office
Email Address: Name@outlook.com
IMAP Server: outlook.office365.com
IMAP Port: 993 Encryption Method: TLS
POP Server: outlook.office365.com
POP Port: 995 Encryption Method: TLS
SMTP Server: smtp-mail.outlook.com
SMTP Port: 587 Encryption Method: STARTTLS
Additional Information:

INTERNET

Network Security/WIFI/Email Server/Software

EMAIL PROVIDER: OUTLOOK/MICROSOFT OFFICE

EMAIL ADDRESS: NAME@OUTLOOK.COM

IMAP SERVER: OUTLOOK.OFFICE365.COM

IMAP PORT: 993 ENCRYPTION METHOD: TLS

POP SERVER: OUTLOOK.OFFICE365.COM

POP PORT: 995 ENCRYPTION METHOD: TLS

SMTP SERVER: SMTP-MAIL.OUTLOOK.COM

SMTP PORT: 587 ENCRYPTION METHOD: STARTTLS

ADDITIONAL INFORMATION:

EMAIL PROVIDER: OUTLOOK/MICROSOFT OFFICE

EMAIL ADDRESS: NAME@OUTLOOK.COM

IMAP SERVER: OUTLOOK.OFFICE365.COM

IMAP PORT: 993 ENCRYPTION METHOD: TLS

POP SERVER: OUTLOOK.OFFICE365.COM

POP PORT: 995 ENCRYPTION METHOD: TLS

SMTP SERVER: SMTP-MAIL.OUTLOOK.COM

SMTP PORT: 587 ENCRYPTION METHOD: STARTTLS

ADDITIONAL INFORMATION:

INTERNET

Network Security/WIFI/Email Server/Software

Email Provider: Outlook/Microsoft Office

Email Address: Name@outlook.com

IMAP Server: outlook.office365.com

IMAP Port: 993 Encryption Method: TLS

POP Server: outlook.office365.com

POP Port: 995 Encryption Method: TLS

SMTP Server: smtp-mail.outlook.com

SMTP Port: 587 Encryption Method: STARTTLS

Additional Information:

Email Provider: Outlook/Microsoft Office

Email Address: Name@outlook.com

IMAP Server: outlook.office365.com

IMAP Port: 993 Encryption Method: TLS

POP Server: outlook.office365.com

POP Port: 995 Encryption Method: TLS

SMTP Server: smtp-mail.outlook.com

SMTP Port: 587 Encryption Method: STARTTLS

Additional Information:

INTERNET

Network Security/WIFI/Email Server/Software

COMPUTER: **MODEL:**

USERNAME:

ADMIN NAME: ADMIN CODE:

PASSWORD:

PASSWORD UPDATES:

DATE:	NEW PASSWORD:

OPERATING SYSTEM:

OS ID:

OS PASSWORD:

ACTIVATION CODE:

NOTES:

CUSTOMER SERVICE:

COMPUTER: **MODEL:**

USERNAME:

ADMIN NAME: ADMIN CODE:

PASSWORD:

PASSWORD UPDATES:

DATE:	NEW PASSWORD:

OPERATING SYSTEM:

OS ID:

OS PASSWORD:

ACTIVATION CODE:

NOTES:

CUSTOMER SERVICE:

COMPUTER: **MODEL:**

USERNAME:

ADMIN NAME: ADMIN CODE:

PASSWORD:

PASSWORD UPDATES:

DATE:	NEW PASSWORD:

OPERATING SYSTEM:

OS ID:

OS PASSWORD:

ACTIVATION CODE:

NOTES:

CUSTOMER SERVICE:

INTERNET

Network Security/WIFI/Email Server/Software

COMPUTER: **MODEL:**

USERNAME:

ADMIN NAME: ADMIN CODE:

PASSWORD:

PASSWORD UPDATES:

DATE:	NEW PASSWORD:

OPERATING SYSTEM:

OS ID:

OS PASSWORD:

ACTIVATION CODE:

NOTES:

CUSTOMER SERVICE:

COMPUTER: **MODEL:**

USERNAME:

ADMIN NAME: ADMIN CODE:

PASSWORD:

PASSWORD UPDATES:

DATE:	NEW PASSWORD:

OPERATING SYSTEM:

OS ID:

OS PASSWORD:

ACTIVATION CODE:

NOTES:

CUSTOMER SERVICE:

COMPUTER: **MODEL:**

USERNAME:

ADMIN NAME: ADMIN CODE:

PASSWORD:

PASSWORD UPDATES:

DATE:	NEW PASSWORD:

OPERATING SYSTEM:

OS ID:

OS PASSWORD:

ACTIVATION CODE:

NOTES:

CUSTOMER SERVICE:

INTERNET

Network Security/WIFI/Email Server/Software

COMPUTER: **MODEL:**

USERNAME:

ADMIN NAME: ADMIN CODE:

PASSWORD:

Password Updates: Date:	New Password:

Operating system:

OS ID:

OS Password:

activation code:

Notes:

Customer Service:

COMPUTER: **MODEL:**

USERNAME:

ADMIN NAME: ADMIN CODE:

PASSWORD:

Password Updates: Date:	New Password:

Operating system:

OS ID:

OS Password:

activation code:

Notes:

Customer Service:

COMPUTER: **MODEL:**

USERNAME:

ADMIN NAME: ADMIN CODE:

PASSWORD:

Password Updates: Date:	New Password:

Operating system:

OS ID:

OS Password:

activation code:

Notes:

Customer Service:

INTERNET

Network Security/WIFI/Email Server/Software

COMPUTER: **MODEL:**

USERNAME:

ADMIN NAME: ADMIN CODE:

PASSWORD:

PASSWORD UPDATES:

DATE:	NEW PASSWORD:

OPERATING SYSTEM:

OS ID:

OS PASSWORD:

ACTIVATION CODE:

NOTES:

CUSTOMER SERVICE:

COMPUTER: **MODEL:**

USERNAME:

ADMIN NAME: ADMIN CODE:

PASSWORD:

PASSWORD UPDATES:

DATE:	NEW PASSWORD:

OPERATING SYSTEM:

OS ID:

OS PASSWORD:

ACTIVATION CODE:

NOTES:

CUSTOMER SERVICE:

COMPUTER: **MODEL:**

USERNAME:

ADMIN NAME: ADMIN CODE:

PASSWORD:

PASSWORD UPDATES:

DATE:	NEW PASSWORD:

OPERATING SYSTEM:

OS ID:

OS PASSWORD:

ACTIVATION CODE:

NOTES:

CUSTOMER SERVICE:

INTERNET

Network Security/WIFI/Email Server/Software

COMPUTER: **MODEL:**

USERNAME:

ADMIN NAME: ADMIN CODE:

PASSWORD:

Password Updates: Date:	New Password:

OPERATING SYSTEM:

OS ID:

OS PASSWORD:

ACTIVATION CODE:

NOTES:

CUSTOMER SERVICE:

COMPUTER: **MODEL:**

USERNAME:

ADMIN NAME: ADMIN CODE:

PASSWORD:

Password Updates: Date:	New Password:

OPERATING SYSTEM:

OS ID:

OS PASSWORD:

ACTIVATION CODE:

NOTES:

CUSTOMER SERVICE:

COMPUTER: **MODEL:**

USERNAME:

ADMIN NAME: ADMIN CODE:

PASSWORD:

Password Updates: Date:	New Password:

OPERATING SYSTEM:

OS ID:

OS PASSWORD:

ACTIVATION CODE:

NOTES:

CUSTOMER SERVICE:

INTERNET

Network Security/WIFI/Email Server/Software

COMPUTER: **MODEL:**

USERNAME:

ADMIN NAME: ADMIN CODE:

PASSWORD:

PASSWORD UPDATES:

DATE:	NEW PASSWORD:

OPERATING SYSTEM:

OS ID:

OS PASSWORD:

ACTIVATION CODE:

NOTES:

CUSTOMER SERVICE:

COMPUTER: **MODEL:**

USERNAME:

ADMIN NAME: ADMIN CODE:

PASSWORD:

PASSWORD UPDATES:

DATE:	NEW PASSWORD:

OPERATING SYSTEM:

OS ID:

OS PASSWORD:

ACTIVATION CODE:

NOTES:

CUSTOMER SERVICE:

COMPUTER: **MODEL:**

USERNAME:

ADMIN NAME: ADMIN CODE:

PASSWORD:

PASSWORD UPDATES:

DATE:	NEW PASSWORD:

OPERATING SYSTEM:

OS ID:

OS PASSWORD:

ACTIVATION CODE:

NOTES:

CUSTOMER SERVICE:

INTERNET

Network Security/WIFI/Email Server/Software

COMPUTER: **MODEL:**

USERNAME:

ADMIN NAME: ADMIN CODE:

PASSWORD:

PASSWORD UPDATES: DATE:	NEW PASSWORD:

OPERATING SYSTEM:

OS ID:

OS PASSWORD:

ACTIVATION CODE:

NOTES:

CUSTOMER SERVICE:

COMPUTER: **MODEL:**

USERNAME:

ADMIN NAME: ADMIN CODE:

PASSWORD:

PASSWORD UPDATES: DATE:	NEW PASSWORD:

OPERATING SYSTEM:

OS ID:

OS PASSWORD:

ACTIVATION CODE:

NOTES:

CUSTOMER SERVICE:

COMPUTER: **MODEL:**

USERNAME:

ADMIN NAME: ADMIN CODE:

PASSWORD:

PASSWORD UPDATES: DATE:	NEW PASSWORD:

OPERATING SYSTEM:

OS ID:

OS PASSWORD:

ACTIVATION CODE:

NOTES:

CUSTOMER SERVICE:

INTERNET

Network Security/WIFI/Email Server/Software

COMPUTER: **MODEL:**

USERNAME:

ADMIN NAME: ADMIN CODE:

PASSWORD:

PASSWORD UPDATES: DATE:	NEW PASSWORD:	OPERATING SYSTEM:
		OS ID:
		OS PASSWORD:
		ACTIVATION CODE:
		NOTES:

CUSTOMER SERVICE:

COMPUTER: **MODEL:**

USERNAME:

ADMIN NAME: ADMIN CODE:

PASSWORD:

PASSWORD UPDATES: DATE:	NEW PASSWORD:	OPERATING SYSTEM:
		OS ID:
		OS PASSWORD:
		ACTIVATION CODE:
		NOTES:

CUSTOMER SERVICE:

COMPUTER: **MODEL:**

USERNAME:

ADMIN NAME: ADMIN CODE:

PASSWORD:

PASSWORD UPDATES: DATE:	NEW PASSWORD:	OPERATING SYSTEM:
		OS ID:
		OS PASSWORD:
		ACTIVATION CODE:
		NOTES:

CUSTOMER SERVICE:

INTERNET

Network Security/WIFI/Email Server/Software

Computer: **Model:**

Username:

Admin Name: Admin Code:

Password:

Password Updates: Date:	New Password:

Operating system:

OS ID:

OS Password:

activation code:

Notes:

Customer Service:

Computer: **Model:**

Username:

Admin Name: Admin Code:

Password:

Password Updates: Date:	New Password:

Operating system:

OS ID:

OS Password:

activation code:

Notes:

Customer Service:

Computer: **Model:**

Username:

Admin Name: Admin Code:

Password:

Password Updates: Date:	New Password:

Operating system:

OS ID:

OS Password:

activation code:

Notes:

Customer Service:

INTERNET

Network Security/WIFI/Email Server/Software

COMPUTER: **MODEL:**

USERNAME:

ADMIN NAME: ADMIN CODE:

PASSWORD:

PASSWORD UPDATES:

DATE:	NEW PASSWORD:

OPERATING SYSTEM:

OS ID:

OS PASSWORD:

ACTIVATION CODE:

NOTES:

CUSTOMER SERVICE:

COMPUTER: **MODEL:**

USERNAME:

ADMIN NAME: ADMIN CODE:

PASSWORD:

PASSWORD UPDATES:

DATE:	NEW PASSWORD:

OPERATING SYSTEM:

OS ID:

OS PASSWORD:

ACTIVATION CODE:

NOTES:

CUSTOMER SERVICE:

COMPUTER: **MODEL:**

USERNAME:

ADMIN NAME: ADMIN CODE:

PASSWORD:

PASSWORD UPDATES:

DATE:	NEW PASSWORD:

OPERATING SYSTEM:

OS ID:

OS PASSWORD:

ACTIVATION CODE:

NOTES:

CUSTOMER SERVICE:

INTERNET

Network Security/WIFI/Email Server/Software

COMPUTER: **MODEL:**

USERNAME:

ADMIN NAME: ADMIN CODE:

PASSWORD:

Password Updates:

Date:	New Password:

Operating system:

OS ID:

OS Password:

activation code:

Notes:

Customer Service:

COMPUTER: **MODEL:**

USERNAME:

ADMIN NAME: ADMIN CODE:

PASSWORD:

Password Updates:

Date:	New Password:

Operating system:

OS ID:

OS Password:

activation code:

Notes:

Customer Service:

COMPUTER: **MODEL:**

USERNAME:

ADMIN NAME: ADMIN CODE:

PASSWORD:

Password Updates:

Date:	New Password:

Operating system:

OS ID:

OS Password:

activation code:

Notes:

Customer Service:

INTERNET

Network Security/WIFI/Email Server/Software

COMPUTER: **MODEL:**

USERNAME:

ADMIN NAME: ADMIN CODE:

PASSWORD:

Password Updates: Date:	New Password:

Operating system:

OS ID:

OS Password:

activation code:

Notes:

Customer Service:

COMPUTER: **MODEL:**

USERNAME:

ADMIN NAME: ADMIN CODE:

PASSWORD:

Password Updates: Date:	New Password:

Operating system:

OS ID:

OS Password:

activation code:

Notes:

Customer Service:

COMPUTER: **MODEL:**

USERNAME:

ADMIN NAME: ADMIN CODE:

PASSWORD:

Password Updates: Date:	New Password:

Operating system:

OS ID:

OS Password:

activation code:

Notes:

Customer Service:

INTERNET

Network Security/WIFI/Email Server/Software

Software:

Username:

Activation/License:

Password:

Password Updates: Date:	New Password:

Date of Purchase: Renewal ☐ Lifetime ☐

Renewal Date: Auto Re-New ☐

Renewal Fee:

Card Assigned:

Notes:

Customer Service:

Software:

Username:

Activation/License:

Password:

Password Updates: Date:	New Password:

Date of Purchase: Renewal ☐ Lifetime ☐

Renewal Date: Auto Re-New ☐

Renewal Fee:

Card Assigned:

Notes:

Customer Service:

Software:

Username:

Activation/License:

Password:

Password Updates: Date:	New Password:

Date of Purchase: Renewal ☐ Lifetime ☐

Renewal Date: Auto Re-New ☐

Renewal Fee:

Card Assigned:

Notes:

Customer Service:

INTERNET

Network Security/WIFI/Email Server/Software

Software:

Username:

Activation/License:

Password:

Password Updates: Date:	New Password:

Date of Purchase: Renewal ☐ Lifetime ☐

Renewal Date: Auto Re-New ☐

Renewal Fee:

Card Assigned:

Notes:

Customer Service:

Software:

Username:

Activation/License:

Password:

Password Updates: Date:	New Password:

Date of Purchase: Renewal ☐ Lifetime ☐

Renewal Date: Auto Re-New ☐

Renewal Fee:

Card Assigned:

Notes:

Customer Service:

Software:

Username:

Activation/License:

Password:

Password Updates: Date:	New Password:

Date of Purchase: Renewal ☐ Lifetime ☐

Renewal Date: Auto Re-New ☐

Renewal Fee:

Card Assigned:

Notes:

Customer Service:

INTERNET

Network Security/WIFI/Email Server/Software

Software:

Username:

Activation/License:

Password:

Password Updates: Date:	New Password:	Date of Purchase:	Renewal ☐	Lifetime ☐
		Renewal Date:	Auto Re-New ☐	
		Renewal Fee:		
		Card Assigned:		
		Notes:		

Customer Service:

Software:

Username:

Activation/License:

Password:

Password Updates: Date:	New Password:	Date of Purchase:	Renewal ☐	Lifetime ☐
		Renewal Date:	Auto Re-New ☐	
		Renewal Fee:		
		Card Assigned:		
		Notes:		

Customer Service:

Software:

Username:

Activation/License:

Password:

Password Updates: Date:	New Password:	Date of Purchase:	Renewal ☐	Lifetime ☐
		Renewal Date:	Auto Re-New ☐	
		Renewal Fee:		
		Card Assigned:		
		Notes:		

Customer Service:

INTERNET

Network Security/WIFI/Email Server/Software

SOFTWARE:

USERNAME:

ACTIVATION/LICENSE:

PASSWORD:

PASSWORD UPDATES:

DATE:	NEW PASSWORD:

DATE OF PURCHASE: RENEWAL ☐ LIFETIME ☐

RENEWAL DATE: AUTO RE-NEW ☐

RENEWAL FEE:

CARD ASSIGNED:

NOTES:

CUSTOMER SERVICE:

SOFTWARE:

USERNAME:

ACTIVATION/LICENSE:

PASSWORD:

PASSWORD UPDATES:

DATE:	NEW PASSWORD:

DATE OF PURCHASE: RENEWAL ☐ LIFETIME ☐

RENEWAL DATE: AUTO RE-NEW ☐

RENEWAL FEE:

CARD ASSIGNED:

NOTES:

CUSTOMER SERVICE:

SOFTWARE:

USERNAME:

ACTIVATION/LICENSE:

PASSWORD:

PASSWORD UPDATES:

DATE:	NEW PASSWORD:

DATE OF PURCHASE: RENEWAL ☐ LIFETIME ☐

RENEWAL DATE: AUTO RE-NEW ☐

RENEWAL FEE:

CARD ASSIGNED:

NOTES:

CUSTOMER SERVICE:

INTERNET

Network Security/WIFI/Email Server/Software

Software:

Username:

Activation/License:

Password:

Password Updates:

Date:	New Password:

Date of Purchase: Renewal ☐ Lifetime ☐

Renewal Date: Auto Re-New ☐

Renewal Fee:

Card Assigned:

Notes:

Customer Service:

Software:

Username:

Activation/License:

Password:

Password Updates:

Date:	New Password:

Date of Purchase: Renewal ☐ Lifetime ☐

Renewal Date: Auto Re-New ☐

Renewal Fee:

Card Assigned:

Notes:

Customer Service:

Software:

Username:

Activation/License:

Password:

Password Updates:

Date:	New Password:

Date of Purchase: Renewal ☐ Lifetime ☐

Renewal Date: Auto Re-New ☐

Renewal Fee:

Card Assigned:

Notes:

Customer Service:

INTERNET

Network Security/WIFI/Email Server/Software

Software:

Username:

Activation/License:

Password:

Password Updates:

Date:	New Password:

Date of Purchase: Renewal ☐ Lifetime ☐

Renewal Date: Auto Re-New ☐

Renewal Fee:

Card Assigned:

Notes:

Customer Service:

Software:

Username:

Activation/License:

Password:

Password Updates:

Date:	New Password:

Date of Purchase: Renewal ☐ Lifetime ☐

Renewal Date: Auto Re-New ☐

Renewal Fee:

Card Assigned:

Notes:

Customer Service:

Software:

Username:

Activation/License:

Password:

Password Updates:

Date:	New Password:

Date of Purchase: Renewal ☐ Lifetime ☐

Renewal Date: Auto Re-New ☐

Renewal Fee:

Card Assigned:

Notes:

Customer Service:

INTERNET

Network Security/WIFI/Email Server/Software

Software:

Username:

Activation/License:

Password:

Date:	New Password:

Password Updates:

Customer Service:

Date of Purchase: Renewal ☐ Lifetime ☐

Renewal Date: Auto Re-New ☐

Renewal Fee:

Card Assigned:

Notes:

Software:

Username:

Activation/License:

Password:

Date:	New Password:

Password Updates:

Customer Service:

Date of Purchase: Renewal ☐ Lifetime ☐

Renewal Date: Auto Re-New ☐

Renewal Fee:

Card Assigned:

Notes:

Software:

Username:

Activation/License:

Password:

Date:	New Password:

Password Updates:

Customer Service:

Date of Purchase: Renewal ☐ Lifetime ☐

Renewal Date: Auto Re-New ☐

Renewal Fee:

Card Assigned:

Notes:

INTERNET

Network Security/WIFI/Email Server/Software

SOFTWARE:

USERNAME:

ACTIVATION/LICENSE:

PASSWORD:

PASSWORD UPDATES:

DATE:	NEW PASSWORD:

DATE OF PURCHASE: RENEWAL ☐ LIFETIME ☐

RENEWAL DATE: AUTO RE-NEW ☐

RENEWAL FEE:

CARD ASSIGNED:

NOTES:

CUSTOMER SERVICE:

SOFTWARE:

USERNAME:

ACTIVATION/LICENSE:

PASSWORD:

PASSWORD UPDATES:

DATE:	NEW PASSWORD:

DATE OF PURCHASE: RENEWAL ☐ LIFETIME ☐

RENEWAL DATE: AUTO RE-NEW ☐

RENEWAL FEE:

CARD ASSIGNED:

NOTES:

CUSTOMER SERVICE:

SOFTWARE:

USERNAME:

ACTIVATION/LICENSE:

PASSWORD:

PASSWORD UPDATES:

DATE:	NEW PASSWORD:

DATE OF PURCHASE: RENEWAL ☐ LIFETIME ☐

RENEWAL DATE: AUTO RE-NEW ☐

RENEWAL FEE:

CARD ASSIGNED:

NOTES:

CUSTOMER SERVICE:

INTERNET

Network Security/WIFI/Email Server/Software

SOFTWARE:

USERNAME:

ACTIVATION/LICENSE:

PASSWORD:

PASSWORD UPDATES: Date:	New Password:	
		Date of Purchase: Renewal ☐ Lifetime ☐
		Renewal Date: Auto Re-New ☐
		Renewal Fee:
		Card Assigned:
		Notes:

CUSTOMER SERVICE:

SOFTWARE:

USERNAME:

ACTIVATION/LICENSE:

PASSWORD:

PASSWORD UPDATES: Date:	New Password:	
		Date of Purchase: Renewal ☐ Lifetime ☐
		Renewal Date: Auto Re-New ☐
		Renewal Fee:
		Card Assigned:
		Notes:

CUSTOMER SERVICE:

SOFTWARE:

USERNAME:

ACTIVATION/LICENSE:

PASSWORD:

PASSWORD UPDATES: Date:	New Password:	
		Date of Purchase: Renewal ☐ Lifetime ☐
		Renewal Date: Auto Re-New ☐
		Renewal Fee:
		Card Assigned:
		Notes:

CUSTOMER SERVICE:

INTERNET

Network Security/WIFI/Email Server/Software

SOFTWARE:

USERNAME:

ACTIVATION/LICENSE:

PASSWORD:

PASSWORD UPDATES: DATE:	NEW PASSWORD:

CUSTOMER SERVICE:

DATE OF PURCHASE: RENEWAL ☐ LIFETIME ☐

RENEWAL DATE: AUTO RE-NEW ☐

RENEWAL FEE:

CARD ASSIGNED:

NOTES:

SOFTWARE:

USERNAME:

ACTIVATION/LICENSE:

PASSWORD:

PASSWORD UPDATES: DATE:	NEW PASSWORD:

CUSTOMER SERVICE:

DATE OF PURCHASE: RENEWAL ☐ LIFETIME ☐

RENEWAL DATE: AUTO RE-NEW ☐

RENEWAL FEE:

CARD ASSIGNED:

NOTES:

SOFTWARE:

USERNAME:

ACTIVATION/LICENSE:

PASSWORD:

PASSWORD UPDATES: DATE:	NEW PASSWORD:

CUSTOMER SERVICE:

DATE OF PURCHASE: RENEWAL ☐ LIFETIME ☐

RENEWAL DATE: AUTO RE-NEW ☐

RENEWAL FEE:

CARD ASSIGNED:

NOTES:

INTERNET

Network Security/WIFI/Email Server/Software

SOFTWARE:

USERNAME:

ACTIVATION/LICENSE:

PASSWORD:

Password Updates: Date:	New Password:

Date of Purchase: Renewal ☐ Lifetime ☐

Renewal Date: Auto Re-New ☐

Renewal Fee:

Card Assigned:

Notes:

Customer Service:

SOFTWARE:

USERNAME:

ACTIVATION/LICENSE:

PASSWORD:

Password Updates: Date:	New Password:

Date of Purchase: Renewal ☐ Lifetime ☐

Renewal Date: Auto Re-New ☐

Renewal Fee:

Card Assigned:

Notes:

Customer Service:

SOFTWARE:

USERNAME:

ACTIVATION/LICENSE:

PASSWORD:

Password Updates: Date:	New Password:

Date of Purchase: Renewal ☐ Lifetime ☐

Renewal Date: Auto Re-New ☐

Renewal Fee:

Card Assigned:

Notes:

Customer Service:

INTERNET

Network Security/WIFI/Email Server/Software

SOFTWARE:

USERNAME:

ACTIVATION/LICENSE:

PASSWORD:

PASSWORD UPDATES: DATE:	NEW PASSWORD:

DATE OF PURCHASE: RENEWAL ☐ LIFETIME ☐

RENEWAL DATE: AUTO RE-NEW ☐

RENEWAL FEE:

CARD ASSIGNED:

NOTES:

CUSTOMER SERVICE:

SOFTWARE:

USERNAME:

ACTIVATION/LICENSE:

PASSWORD:

PASSWORD UPDATES: DATE:	NEW PASSWORD:

DATE OF PURCHASE: RENEWAL ☐ LIFETIME ☐

RENEWAL DATE: AUTO RE-NEW ☐

RENEWAL FEE:

CARD ASSIGNED:

NOTES:

CUSTOMER SERVICE:

SOFTWARE:

USERNAME:

ACTIVATION/LICENSE:

PASSWORD:

PASSWORD UPDATES: DATE:	NEW PASSWORD:

DATE OF PURCHASE: RENEWAL ☐ LIFETIME ☐

RENEWAL DATE: AUTO RE-NEW ☐

RENEWAL FEE:

CARD ASSIGNED:

NOTES:

CUSTOMER SERVICE:

INTERNET

Network Security/WIFI/Email Server/Software

SOFTWARE:

USERNAME:

ACTIVATION/LICENSE:

PASSWORD:

PASSWORD UPDATES: DATE:	NEW PASSWORD:

DATE OF PURCHASE: RENEWAL ☐ LIFETIME ☐

RENEWAL DATE: AUTO RE-NEW ☐

RENEWAL FEE:

CARD ASSIGNED:

NOTES:

CUSTOMER SERVICE:

SOFTWARE:

USERNAME:

ACTIVATION/LICENSE:

PASSWORD:

PASSWORD UPDATES: DATE:	NEW PASSWORD:

DATE OF PURCHASE: RENEWAL ☐ LIFETIME ☐

RENEWAL DATE: AUTO RE-NEW ☐

RENEWAL FEE:

CARD ASSIGNED:

NOTES:

CUSTOMER SERVICE:

SOFTWARE:

USERNAME:

ACTIVATION/LICENSE:

PASSWORD:

PASSWORD UPDATES: DATE:	NEW PASSWORD:

DATE OF PURCHASE: RENEWAL ☐ LIFETIME ☐

RENEWAL DATE: AUTO RE-NEW ☐

RENEWAL FEE:

CARD ASSIGNED:

NOTES:

CUSTOMER SERVICE:

INTERNET

Network Security/WIFI/Email Server/Software

SOFTWARE:

USERNAME:

ACTIVATION/LICENSE:

PASSWORD:

PASSWORD UPDATES: Date:	New Password:

DATE OF PURCHASE: RENEWAL ☐ LIFETIME ☐

RENEWAL DATE: AUTO RE-NEW ☐

RENEWAL FEE:

CARD ASSIGNED:

NOTES:

CUSTOMER SERVICE:

SOFTWARE:

USERNAME:

ACTIVATION/LICENSE:

PASSWORD:

PASSWORD UPDATES: Date:	New Password:

DATE OF PURCHASE: RENEWAL ☐ LIFETIME ☐

RENEWAL DATE: AUTO RE-NEW ☐

RENEWAL FEE:

CARD ASSIGNED:

NOTES:

CUSTOMER SERVICE:

SOFTWARE:

USERNAME:

ACTIVATION/LICENSE:

PASSWORD:

PASSWORD UPDATES: Date:	New Password:

DATE OF PURCHASE: RENEWAL ☐ LIFETIME ☐

RENEWAL DATE: AUTO RE-NEW ☐

RENEWAL FEE:

CARD ASSIGNED:

NOTES:

CUSTOMER SERVICE:

Crypto Wallet & NFT Tracker

CRYPTO NFT

INTERNET

Crypto Wallet & NFT Tracker

WALLET: OPEN DATE: / /

WEBSITE:

USERNAME:

EMAIL USED:

WALLET ADDRESS:

PUBLIC KEY:

PRIVATE KEY: PIN:

PASSWORD:

PASSWORD UPDATES:

DATE:	NEW PASSWORD:

SECRET QUESTION:

ANSWER:

SECRET QUESTION:

ANSWER:

SECRET QUESTION:

ANSWER:

RECOVERY SEED WORD PHRASES:

NOTES:

INTERNET

Crypto Wallet & NFT Tracker

Crypto tracker

Date	Buy/Sell	Amount	Coin	Notes

CRYPTO NFT

INTERNET

Crypto Wallet & NFT Tracker

WALLET: OPEN DATE: / /

WEBSITE:

USERNAME:

EMAIL USED:

WALLET ADDRESS:

PUBLIC KEY:

PRIVATE KEY: PIN:

PASSWORD:

PASSWORD UPDATES:

DATE:	NEW PASSWORD:

SECRET QUESTION:

ANSWER:

SECRET QUESTION:

ANSWER:

SECRET QUESTION:

ANSWER:

RECOVERY SEED WORD PHRASES:

NOTES:

INTERNET
Crypto Wallet & NFT Tracker

Crypto tracker

Date	Buy/Sell	Amount	Coin	Notes

CRYPTO NFT

INTERNET

Crypto Wallet & NFT Tracker

WALLET: **OPEN DATE: / /**

WEBSITE:

USERNAME:

EMAIL USED:

WALLET ADDRESS:

PUBLIC KEY:

PRIVATE KEY: PIN:

PASSWORD:

PASSWORD UPDATES:

DATE:	NEW PASSWORD:

SECRET QUESTION:

ANSWER:

SECRET QUESTION:

ANSWER:

SECRET QUESTION:

ANSWER:

RECOVERY SEED WORD PHRASES:

NOTES:

INTERNET

Crypto Wallet & NFT Tracker

Crypto tracker

Date	Buy/Sell	Amount	Coin	Notes

INTERNET

Crypto Wallet & NFT Tracker

WALLET: **OPEN DATE:** / /

WEBSITE:

USERNAME:

EMAIL USED:

WALLET ADDRESS:

PUBLIC KEY:

PRIVATE KEY: PIN:

PASSWORD:

PASSWORD UPDATES:

DATE:	NEW PASSWORD:

SECRET QUESTION:

ANSWER:

SECRET QUESTION:

ANSWER:

SECRET QUESTION:

ANSWER:

RECOVERY SEED WORD PHRASES:

NOTES:

INTERNET

Crypto Wallet & NFT Tracker

Crypto tracker

Date	Buy/Sell	Amount	Coin	Notes

INTERNET
Crypto Wallet & NFT Tracker

WALLET: **OPEN DATE: / /**

WEBSITE:

USERNAME:

EMAIL USED:

WALLET ADDRESS:

PUBLIC KEY:

PRIVATE KEY: PIN:

PASSWORD:

Password Updates:

Date:	New Password:	
		Secret Question:
		Answer:
		Secret Question:
		Answer:
		Secret Question:
		Answer:

RECOVERY SEED WORD PHRASES:

NOTES:

INTERNET

Crypto Wallet & NFT Tracker

Crypto tracker

Date	Buy/Sell	Amount	Coin	Notes

CRYPTO NFT

INTERNET

Crypto Wallet & NFT Tracker

Wallet: **Open Date:** / /

Website:

Username:

Email Used:

Wallet Address:

Public Key:

Private Key: PIN:

Password:

Password Updates:

Date:	New Password:

Secret Question:

Answer:

Secret Question:

Answer:

Secret Question:

Answer:

Recovery Seed Word Phrases:

Notes:

INTERNET
Crypto Wallet & NFT Tracker

Crypto tracker

Date	Buy/Sell	Amount	Coin	Notes

CRYPTO NFT

INTERNET

Crypto Wallet & NFT Tracker

WALLET: **OPEN DATE: / /**

WEBSITE:

USERNAME:

EMAIL USED:

WALLET ADDRESS:

PUBLIC KEY:

PRIVATE KEY: PIN:

PASSWORD:

PASSWORD UPDATES:

DATE:	NEW PASSWORD:

SECRET QUESTION:

ANSWER:

SECRET QUESTION:

ANSWER:

SECRET QUESTION:

ANSWER:

RECOVERY SEED WORD PHRASES:

NOTES:

INTERNET
Crypto Wallet & NFT Tracker

CRYPTO TRACKER

DATE	BUY/SELL	AMOUNT	COIN	NOTES

INTERNET

Crypto Wallet & NFT Tracker

NFT TRACKER

Wallet Platform token art/item Transaction $ + gas

Date Profit/Loss Notes

Wallet Platform token art/item Transaction $ + gas

Date Profit/Loss Notes

Wallet Platform token art/item Transaction $ + gas

Date Profit/Loss Notes

Wallet Platform token art/item Transaction $ + gas

Date Profit/Loss Notes

Wallet Platform token art/item Transaction $ + gas

Date Profit/Loss Notes

Wallet Platform token art/item Transaction $ + gas

Date Profit/Loss Notes

Wallet Platform token art/item Transaction $ + gas

Date Profit/Loss Notes

Wallet Platform token art/item Transaction $ + gas

Date Profit/Loss Notes

Wallet Platform token art/item Transaction $ + gas

Date Profit/Loss Notes

INTERNET
Crypto Wallet & NFT Tracker

NFT TRACKER

WALLET PLATFORM TOKEN ART/ITEM TRANSACTION $ + GAS

DATE PROFIT/LOSS NOTES

WALLET PLATFORM TOKEN ART/ITEM TRANSACTION $ + GAS

DATE PROFIT/LOSS NOTES

WALLET PLATFORM TOKEN ART/ITEM TRANSACTION $ + GAS

DATE PROFIT/LOSS NOTES

WALLET PLATFORM TOKEN ART/ITEM TRANSACTION $ + GAS

DATE PROFIT/LOSS NOTES

WALLET PLATFORM TOKEN ART/ITEM TRANSACTION $ + GAS

DATE PROFIT/LOSS NOTES

WALLET PLATFORM TOKEN ART/ITEM TRANSACTION $ + GAS

DATE PROFIT/LOSS NOTES

WALLET PLATFORM TOKEN ART/ITEM TRANSACTION $ + GAS

DATE PROFIT/LOSS NOTES

WALLET PLATFORM TOKEN ART/ITEM TRANSACTION $ + GAS

DATE PROFIT/LOSS NOTES

WALLET PLATFORM TOKEN ART/ITEM TRANSACTION $ + GAS

DATE PROFIT/LOSS NOTES

INTERNET
Crypto Wallet & NFT Tracker

NFT TRACKER

Wallet Platform token art/item Transaction $ + gas

Date Profit/Loss Notes

Wallet Platform token art/item Transaction $ + gas

Date Profit/Loss Notes

Wallet Platform token art/item Transaction $ + gas

Date Profit/Loss Notes

Wallet Platform token art/item Transaction $ + gas

Date Profit/Loss Notes

Wallet Platform token art/item Transaction $ + gas

Date Profit/Loss Notes

Wallet Platform token art/item Transaction $ + gas

Date Profit/Loss Notes

Wallet Platform token art/item Transaction $ + gas

Date Profit/Loss Notes

Wallet Platform token art/item Transaction $ + gas

Date Profit/Loss Notes

Wallet Platform token art/item Transaction $ + gas

Date Profit/Loss Notes

INTERNET
Crypto Wallet & NFT Tracker

NFT TRACKER

Wallet Platform token art/item Transaction $ + gas

Date Profit/Loss Notes

Wallet Platform token art/item Transaction $ + gas

Date Profit/Loss Notes

Wallet Platform token art/item Transaction $ + gas

Date Profit/Loss Notes

Wallet Platform token art/item Transaction $ + gas

Date Profit/Loss Notes

Wallet Platform token art/item Transaction $ + gas

Date Profit/Loss Notes

Wallet Platform token art/item Transaction $ + gas

Date Profit/Loss Notes

Wallet Platform token art/item Transaction $ + gas

Date Profit/Loss Notes

Wallet Platform token art/item Transaction $ + gas

Date Profit/Loss Notes

Wallet Platform token art/item Transaction $ + gas

Date Profit/Loss Notes

INTERNET

Crypto Wallet & NFT Tracker

NFT TRACKER

Wallet Platform token art/item Transaction $ + gas

Date Profit/Loss Notes

Wallet Platform token art/item Transaction $ + gas

Date Profit/Loss Notes

Wallet Platform token art/item Transaction $ + gas

Date Profit/Loss Notes

Wallet Platform token art/item Transaction $ + gas

Date Profit/Loss Notes

Wallet Platform token art/item Transaction $ + gas

Date Profit/Loss Notes

Wallet Platform token art/item Transaction $ + gas

Date Profit/Loss Notes

Wallet Platform token art/item Transaction $ + gas

Date Profit/Loss Notes

Wallet Platform token art/item Transaction $ + gas

Date Profit/Loss Notes

Wallet Platform token art/item Transaction $ + gas

Date Profit/Loss Notes

INTERNET

Crypto Wallet & NFT Tracker

NFT TRACKER

Wallet Platform token art/item Transaction $ + gas

Date Profit/Loss Notes

Wallet Platform token art/item Transaction $ + gas

Date Profit/Loss Notes

Wallet Platform token art/item Transaction $ + gas

Date Profit/Loss Notes

Wallet Platform token art/item Transaction $ + gas

Date Profit/Loss Notes

Wallet Platform token art/item Transaction $ + gas

Date Profit/Loss Notes

Wallet Platform token art/item Transaction $ + gas

Date Profit/Loss Notes

Wallet Platform token art/item Transaction $ + gas

Date Profit/Loss Notes

Wallet Platform token art/item Transaction $ + gas

Date Profit/Loss Notes

Wallet Platform token art/item Transaction $ + gas

Date Profit/Loss Notes

INTERNET

Crypto Wallet & NFT Tracker

NFT TRACKER

Wallet Platform token art/item Transaction $ + gas

Date Profit/Loss Notes

Wallet Platform token art/item Transaction $ + gas

Date Profit/Loss Notes

Wallet Platform token art/item Transaction $ + gas

Date Profit/Loss Notes

Wallet Platform token art/item Transaction $ + gas

Date Profit/Loss Notes

Wallet Platform token art/item Transaction $ + gas

Date Profit/Loss Notes

Wallet Platform token art/item Transaction $ + gas

Date Profit/Loss Notes

Wallet Platform token art/item Transaction $ + gas

Date Profit/Loss Notes

Wallet Platform token art/item Transaction $ + gas

Date Profit/Loss Notes

Wallet Platform token art/item Transaction $ + gas

Date Profit/Loss Notes

INTERNET
Crypto Wallet & NFT Tracker

NFT TRACKER

Wallet Platform token art/item Transaction $ + gas

Date Profit/Loss Notes

Wallet Platform token art/item Transaction $ + gas

Date Profit/Loss Notes

Wallet Platform token art/item Transaction $ + gas

Date Profit/Loss Notes

Wallet Platform token art/item Transaction $ + gas

Date Profit/Loss Notes

Wallet Platform token art/item Transaction $ + gas

Date Profit/Loss Notes

Wallet Platform token art/item Transaction $ + gas

Date Profit/Loss Notes

Wallet Platform token art/item Transaction $ + gas

Date Profit/Loss Notes

Wallet Platform token art/item Transaction $ + gas

Date Profit/Loss Notes

Wallet Platform token art/item Transaction $ + gas

Date Profit/Loss Notes

INTERNET

Crypto Wallet & NFT Tracker

NFT TRACKER

Wallet Platform token art/item Transaction $ + gas

Date Profit/Loss Notes

Wallet Platform token art/item Transaction $ + gas

Date Profit/Loss Notes

Wallet Platform token art/item Transaction $ + gas

Date Profit/Loss Notes

Wallet Platform token art/item Transaction $ + gas

Date Profit/Loss Notes

Wallet Platform token art/item Transaction $ + gas

Date Profit/Loss Notes

Wallet Platform token art/item Transaction $ + gas

Date Profit/Loss Notes

Wallet Platform token art/item Transaction $ + gas

Date Profit/Loss Notes

Wallet Platform token art/item Transaction $ + gas

Date Profit/Loss Notes

Wallet Platform token art/item Transaction $ + gas

Date Profit/Loss Notes

INTERNET

Social Media/Digital Resume/Personal Websites

Social Media	
Username	**Password**

INTERNET

Social Media/Digital Resume/Personal Websites

Social Media

Username	Password

INTERNET

Social Media/Digital Resume/Personal Websites

Social Media

Username	Password

INTERNET

Social Media/Digital Resume/Personal Websites

Digital Presence

To simplify access and sharing, a valuable tip is to create stickers with QR codes for these locations and place them on this page. These can be created using address labels.

Digital Resume Address:

Personal Websites:

INTERNET

Social Media/Digital Resume/Personal Websites

Digital Presence

To simplify access and sharing, a valuable tip is to create stickers with QR codes for these locations and place them on this page. These can be created using address labels.

Digital Resume Address:

Personal Websites:

INTERNET

Social Media/Digital Resume/Personal Websites

Digital Presence

To simplify access and sharing, a valuable tip is to create stickers with QR codes for these locations and place them on this page. These can be created using address labels.

Digital Resume Address:

Personal Websites:

INTERNET

Social Media/Digital Resume/Personal Websites

Digital Presence

To simplify access and sharing, a valuable tip is to create stickers with QR codes for these locations and place them on this page. These can be created using address labels.

Digital Resume Address:

Personal Websites:

IMPORTANT DATES SECTION

Holidays

Some widely accepted holidays or popular holidays are already included. There is also room to add the holidays you like to celebrate and remember.

Birthdays

Put in birthdays that are important to you: your family, friends, co-workers, important figures in your life...

Anniversaries

Don't forget another anniversary. Just jot it down in your musketeer. From weddings to first days, anything goes.

Important Events

Whatever events are important to you, place them in the month they happen. Anytime you change calendrers or jobs, you can easily re-load all of your dates again.

IMPORTANT DATES

Holidays
Birthdays
Anniversaries
Important Events

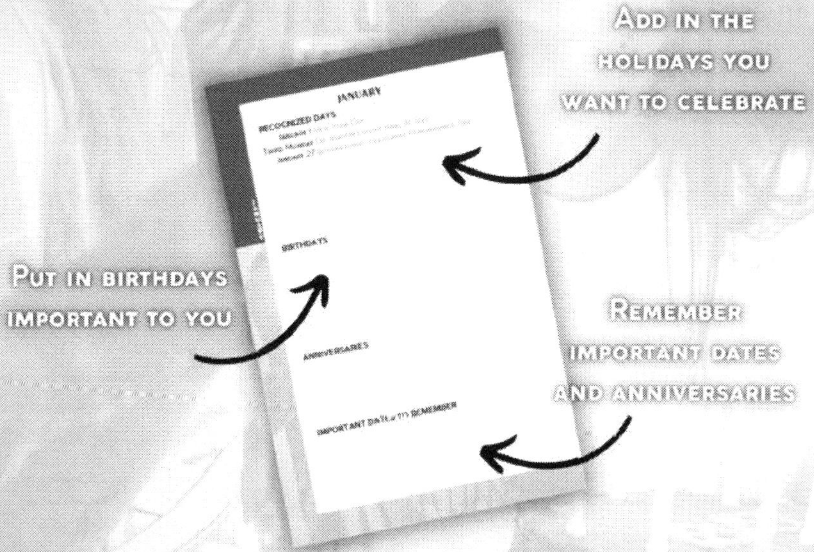

JANUARY

RECOGNIZED DAYS

JANUARY 1 NEW YEAR DAY
THIRD MONDAY DR. MARTIN LUTHER KING JR. DAY
JANUARY 27 INTERNATIONAL HOLOCAUST REMEMBRANCE DAY

BIRTHDAYS

ANNIVERSARIES

IMPORTANT DATES TO REMEMBER

FEBRUARY

RECOGNIZED DAYS

Black History Month

February 1 National Freedom Day
February 14 Valentines Day
February 21 Presidents Day

BIRTHDAYS

ANNIVERSARIES

IMPORTANT DATES TO REMEMBER

MARCH

RECOGNIZED DAYS

Women's History Month

Tuesday b.f. Ash Wednesday	Mardi Gras
46 days b.f. Easter Sunday	Ash Wednesday
Second Sunday	Day light savings begins
March 17	St. Patrick's Day
March 20	Spring Equinox (around the 20th)

BIRTHDAYS

ANNIVERSARIES

IMPORTANT DATES TO REMEMBER

APRIL

RECOGNIZED DAYS

April 1 April Fools Day
April 6 Family Love Day
Sunday b.f. Easter Palm Sunday
Friday b.f. Easter Good Friday
Sunday a.f. 1st full moon of Spring Eqnx Easter
April 15 Tax Day
April 22 Earth Day

BIRTHDAYS

ANNIVERSARIES

IMPORTANT DATES TO REMEMBER

MAY

RECOGNIZED DAYS

May 5	Cinco De Mayo
Second Sunday	Mother's Day
May 30	Memorial Day (Fallen Soldiers)

MAY

BIRTHDAYS

ANNIVERSARIES

IMPORTANT DATES TO REMEMBER

JUNE

RECOGNIZED DAYS

LGBTQ+ Pride Month

June 19 Juneteenth

June 20 Summer Solstice (Around 20th)

BIRTHDAYS

ANNIVERSARIES

IMPORTANT DATES TO REMEMBER

JULY

RECOGNIZED DAYS

JULY 4 INDEPENDENCE DAY

BIRTHDAYS

ANNIVERSARIES

IMPORTANT DATES TO REMEMBER

AUGUST

RECOGNIZED DAYS

BIRTHDAYS

ANNIVERSARIES

IMPORTANT DATES TO REMEMBER

SEPTEMBER

RECOGNIZED DAYS

First Monday Labor Day
September 11 Patriot Day/National Remembrance Day
September 21 International Day of Peace
September 23 Fall Equinox (Around 23rd)

BIRTHDAYS

ANNIVERSARIES

IMPORTANT DATES TO REMEMBER

OCTOBER

RECOGNIZED DAYS

Second Monday Columbus/Native American Day
October 31 Halloween

BIRTHDAYS

ANNIVERSARIES

IMPORTANT DATES TO REMEMBER

NOVEMBER

RECOGNIZED DAYS

November 2 All Souls Day (Day of the Dead)
First Sunday Daylight Savings Ends
November 11 Veterans Day
November 13 World Kindness Day
Fourth Thursday Thanksgiving Day

BIRTHDAYS

ANNIVERSARIES

IMPORTANT DATES TO REMEMBER

DECEMBER

RECOGNIZED DAYS

December 7	Pearl Harbor Remembrance
December 21	Winter Solstice (Around 21st)
December 25	Christmas Day
December 26	Kwanzaa
December 31	New Year Eve

BIRTHDAYS

ANNIVERSARIES

IMPORTANT DATES TO REMEMBER

SCHOOL LIFE SECTION

Highschool
From your GPA to your favorite teachers and student council, and how to reach them. You never know when a good contact will come in handy.

College/Trade School
Make sure you have your best classmates, teachers, GPA, and honors information on hand for future references. Great to have on hand for completing resumes.

Graduate School
With every school you attend, you pick up new contacts. Keep those contacts handy by writing down their email and phone numbers.

Internships
Corporate contacts, co-workers, even students who you were involved with on projects all are great resources in the real world.

Associations
From your Greek affiliation to your clubs and boosters. Keep your contacts for years to come by recording them in you Little Musketeer.

SCHOOL LIFE

Highschool
College/Trade School
Graduate School
Internships
Associations

Keep track of all your school information including GPA and honors

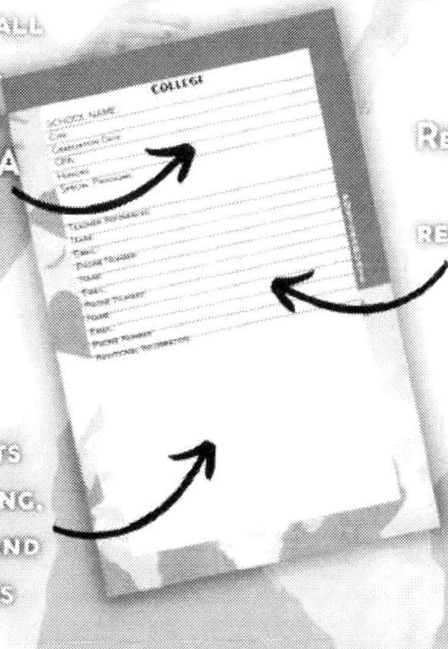

Remember your teacher references and contacts

track contacts for volunteering, associations, and organizations

HIGHSCHOOL

SCHOOL NAME:

City:

Graduation Date:

GPA:

Honors:

Special Programs:

Teacher References:

Name:

Email:

Phone Number:

Name:

Email:

Phone Number:

Name:

Email:

Phone Number:

Additional Information:

HIGHSCHOOL

HIGHSCHOOL

SCHOOL NAME:

City:

Graduation Date:

GPA:

Honors:

Special Programs:

Teacher References:

Name:

Email:

Phone Number:

Name:

Email:

Phone Number:

Name:

Email:

Phone Number:

Additional Information:

TRADE SCHOOL

SCHOOL NAME:

City:

Graduation Date:

GPA:

Honors:

Special Programs:

Teacher References:

Name:

Email:

Phone Number:

Name:

Email:

Phone Number:

Name:

Email:

Phone Number:

Additional Information:

TRADE SCHOOL

SCHOOL NAME:

City:

Graduation Date:

GPA:

Honors:

Special Programs:

Teacher References:

Name:

Email:

Phone Number:

Name:

Email:

Phone Number:

Name:

Email:

Phone Number:

Additional Information:

COLLEGE

SCHOOL NAME:

City:

Graduation Date:

GPA:

Honors:

Special Programs:

Teacher References:

Name:

Email:

Phone Number:

Name:

Email:

Phone Number:

Name:

Email:

Phone Number:

Additional Information:

UNDERGRADUATE

COLLEGE

SCHOOL NAME:

City:

Graduation Date:

GPA:

Honors:

Special Programs:

Teacher References:

Name:

Email:

Phone Number:

Name:

Email:

Phone Number:

Name:

Email:

Phone Number:

Additional Information:

COLLEGE

SCHOOL NAME:

City:

Graduation Date:

GPA:

Honors:

Special Programs:

Teacher References:

Name:

Email:

Phone Number:

Name:

Email:

Phone Number:

Name:

Email:

Phone Number:

Additional Information:

COLLEGE

SCHOOL NAME:

CITY:

GRADUATION DATE:

GPA:

HONORS:

SPECIAL PROGRAMS:

TEACHER REFERENCES:

NAME:

EMAIL:

PHONE NUMBER:

NAME:

EMAIL:

PHONE NUMBER:

NAME:

EMAIL:

PHONE NUMBER:

ADDITIONAL INFORMATION:

COLLEGE

SCHOOL NAME:

City:

Graduation Date:

GPA:

Honors:

Special Programs:

Teacher References:

Name:

Email:

Phone Number:

Name:

Email:

Phone Number:

Name:

Email:

Phone Number:

Additional Information:

COLLEGE

SCHOOL NAME:

CITY:

GRADUATION DATE:

GPA:

HONORS:

SPECIAL PROGRAMS:

TEACHER REFERENCES:

NAME:

EMAIL:

PHONE NUMBER:

NAME:

EMAIL:

PHONE NUMBER:

NAME:

EMAIL:

PHONE NUMBER:

ADDITIONAL INFORMATION:

INTERNSHIPS

Organization:

City:

Participation Dates:

Contribution:

Awards:

Special Programs:

Mentor Role:

Name:

Email:

Phone Number:

Mentor Role:

Name:

Email:

Phone Number:

Mentor Role:

Name:

Email:

Phone Number:

Additional Information:

INTERNSHIPS

Organization:

City:

Participation Dates:

Contribution:

Awards:

Special Programs:

Mentor Role:

Name:

Email:

Phone Number:

Mentor Role:

Name:

Email:

Phone Number:

Mentor Role:

Name:

Email:

Phone Number:

Additional Information:

INTERNSHIPS

Organization:

City:

Participation Dates:

Contribution:

Awards:

Special Programs:

Mentor Role:

Name:

Email:

Phone Number:

Mentor Role:

Name:

Email:

Phone Number:

Mentor Role:

Name:

Email:

Phone Number:

Additional Information:

INTERNSHIPS

Organization:

City:

Participation Dates:

Contribution:

Awards:

Special Programs:

Mentor Role:

Name:

Email:

Phone Number:

Mentor Role:

Name:

Email:

Phone Number:

Mentor Role:

Name:

Email:

Phone Number:

Additional Information:

INTERNSHIPS

Organization:

City:

Participation Dates:

Contribution:

Awards:

Special Programs:

Mentor Role:

Name:

Email:

Phone Number:

Mentor Role:

Name:

Email:

Phone Number:

Mentor Role:

Name:

Email:

Phone Number:

Additional Information:

INTERNSHIPS

Organization:

City:

Participation Dates:

Contribution:

Awards:

Special Programs:

Mentor Role:

Name:

Email:

Phone Number:

Mentor Role:

Name:

Email:

Phone Number:

Mentor Role:

Name:

Email:

Phone Number:

Additional Information:

ASSOCIATIONS

Organization:

Chapter:

Affiliation:

Contribution:

My Role:

Dates Involved:

Special Programs:

Notable members

Name:

Phone:

Email:

Notes:

Notable members

Name:

Phone:

Email:

Notes:

Notable members

Name:

Phone:

Email:

Notes:

ASSOCIATIONS

Organization:

Chapter:

Affiliation:

Contribution:

My Role:

Dates Involved:

Special Programs:

Notable members

Name:

Phone:

Email:

Notes:

Notable members

Name:

Phone:

Email:

Notes:

Notable members

Name:

Phone:

Email:

Notes:

ASSOCIATIONS

Organization:

Chapter:

Affiliation:

Contribution:

My Role:

Dates Involved:

Special Programs:

Notable members

Name:

Phone:

Email:

Notes:

Notable members

Name:

Phone:

Email:

Notes:

Notable members

Name:

Phone:

Email:

Notes:

ASSOCIATIONS

Organization:

Chapter:

Affiliation:

Contribution:

My Role:

Dates Involved:

Special Programs:

Notable members

Name:

Phone:

Email:

Notes:

Notable members

Name:

Phone:

Email:

Notes:

Notable members

Name:

Phone:

Email:

Notes:

ASSOCIATIONS

Organization:

Chapter:

Affiliation:

Contribution:

My Role:

Dates Involved:

Special Programs:

Notable members

Name:

Phone:

Email:

Notes:

Notable members

Name:

Phone:

Email:

Notes:

Notable members

Name:

Phone:

Email:

Notes:

ASSOCIATIONS

Organization:

Chapter:

Affiliation:

Contribution:

My Role:

Dates Involved:

Special Programs:

Notable members

Name:

Phone:

Email:

Notes:

Notable members

Name:

Phone:

Email:

Notes:

Notable members

Name:

Phone:

Email:

Notes:

ASSOCIATIONS

Organization:

Chapter:

Affiliation:

Contribution:

My Role:

Dates Involved:

Special Programs:

Notable members

Name:

Phone:

Email:

Notes:

Notable members

Name:

Phone:

Email:

Notes:

Notable members

Name:

Phone:

Email:

Notes:

ASSOCIATIONS

Organization:

Chapter:

Affiliation:

Contribution:

My Role:

Dates Involved:

Special Programs:

Notable members

Name:

Phone:

Email:

Notes:

Notable members

Name:

Phone:

Email:

Notes:

Notable members

Name:

Phone:

Email:

Notes:

ASSOCIATIONS

Organization:

Chapter:

Affiliation:

Contribution:

My Role:

Dates Involved:

Special Programs:

Notable members

Name:

Phone:

Email:

Notes:

Notable members

Name:

Phone:

Email:

Notes:

Notable members

Name:

Phone:

Email:

Notes:

ASSOCIATIONS

Organization:

Chapter:

Affiliation:

Contribution:

My Role:

Dates Involved:

Special Programs:

Notable members

Name:

Phone:

Email:

Notes:

Notable members

Name:

Phone:

Email:

Notes:

Notable members

Name:

Phone:

Email:

Notes:

HOME LIFE SECTION

Places I've Lived/Neighbors
Keep track of your old address, neighbors, roommates, and how long you lived there. Comes in handy when filling out applications for loans and jobs.

Personal Finances
Keep track of where you bank, and contacts for loans as well as how to report lost or stolen cards.

Subscriptions
Keep track of your subscription services, what card you use to pay for them incase you need to update it and how often it is renewed.

Insurance/Utilities/Inventory
Keep a home inventory, who carries your insurance, and the best contact numbers for your utility providers.

Service Providers
From your family doctor to your favorite babysitter to the plumber you can always reply on. Keep everyone's contact info handy and sharable.

HOME LIFE

Places I've Lived/Neighbors
Personal Finances
Subscriptions
Insurance/Utilities/Inventory
Service Providers

HOME LIFE

Places I've Lived/Neighbors

Address: ______________________ Unit: __________

City: ______________ State: __________ Zip: __________

Country: ______________________________

☐ Alone ☐ With Family ☐ With Roommate(s)

Date Moved In: / / Date Moved Out: / /

Others in the home:

____

____

____

Neighbor:

Name: ______________________________

Children: ______________________________

____

Address: ______________________________

Phone Number: ______________________________

Notes:

Neighbor:

Name: ______________________________

Children: ______________________________

____

Address: ______________________________

Phone Number: ______________________________

Notes:

Neighbor:

Name: ______________________________

Children: ______________________________

____

Address: ______________________________

Phone Number: ______________________________

Notes:

HOME LIFE

Places I've Lived/Neighbors

Address: ______________________ Unit: __________
City: ______________ State: __________ Zip: __________
Country: ______________________________

☐ Alone ☐ With Family ☐ With Roommate(s)

Date Moved In: / / Date Moved Out: / /

Others in the home:

____
____
____

Neighbor:
Name: ______________________________
Children: ______________________________
____
Address: ______________________________
Phone Number: ______________________________
Notes:

Neighbor:
Name: ______________________________
Children: ______________________________
____
Address: ______________________________
Phone Number: ______________________________
Notes:

Neighbor:
Name: ______________________________
Children: ______________________________
____
Address: ______________________________
Phone Number: ______________________________
Notes:

HOME LIFE

Places I've Lived/Neighbors

Address: ______________________ Unit: __________

City: ______________ State: __________ Zip: __________

Country: ______________________

☐ Alone ☐ With Family ☐ With Roommate(s)

Date Moved In: / / Date Moved Out: / /

Others in the home:

____

____

____

Neighbor:

Name: ______________________

Children: ______________________

____

Address: ______________________

Phone Number: ______________________

Notes:

Neighbor:

Name: ______________________

Children: ______________________

____

Address: ______________________

Phone Number: ______________________

Notes:

Neighbor:

Name: ______________________

Children: ______________________

____

Address: ______________________

Phone Number: ______________________

Notes:

HOME LIFE
Places I've Lived/Neighbors

Address: ______________________ Unit: __________
City: ______________ State: __________ Zip: __________
Country: ______________________________

☐ Alone ☐ With Family ☐ With Roommate(s)

Date Moved In: / / Date Moved Out: / /

Others in the home:

____
____
____

Neighbor:
Name: ______________________________
Children: ______________________________
____
Address: ______________________________
Phone Number: ______________________________
Notes:

Neighbor:
Name: ______________________________
Children: ______________________________
____
Address: ______________________________
Phone Number: ______________________________
Notes:

Neighbor:
Name: ______________________________
Children: ______________________________
____
Address: ______________________________
Phone Number: ______________________________
Notes:

HOME LIFE

Places I've Lived/Neighbors

Address: ______________________ Unit: __________

City: ______________ State: __________ Zip: __________

Country: ______________________________

☐ Alone ☐ With Family ☐ With Roommate(s)

Date Moved In: / / Date Moved Out: / /

Others in the home:

____

____

____

Neighbor:

Name: ______________________________

Children: ______________________________

____

Address: ______________________________

Phone Number: ______________________________

Notes:

Neighbor:

Name: ______________________________

Children: ______________________________

____

Address: ______________________________

Phone Number: ______________________________

Notes:

Neighbor:

Name: ______________________________

Children: ______________________________

____

Address: ______________________________

Phone Number: ______________________________

Notes:

HOME LIFE

Places I've Lived/Neighbors

Address: ______________________ Unit: __________
City: ______________ State: __________ Zip: __________
Country: ______________________________
☐ Alone ☐ With Family ☐ With Roommate(s)
Date Moved In: / / Date Moved Out: / /
Others in the home:

____
____
____

Neighbor:
Name: ______________________________
Children: ______________________________
____
Address: ______________________________
Phone Number: ______________________________
Notes:

Neighbor:
Name: ______________________________
Children: ______________________________
____
Address: ______________________________
Phone Number: ______________________________
Notes:

Neighbor:
Name: ______________________________
Children: ______________________________
____
Address: ______________________________
Phone Number: ______________________________
Notes:

HOME LIFE

Places I've Lived/Neighbors

Address: ______________________ Unit: __________

City: ______________ State: __________ Zip: __________

Country: ______________________

☐ Alone ☐ With Family ☐ With Roommate(s)

Date Moved In: / / Date Moved Out: / /

Others in the home:

____

____

____

Neighbor:

Name: ______________________

Children: ______________________

____

Address: ______________________

Phone Number: ______________________

Notes:

Neighbor:

Name: ______________________

Children: ______________________

____

Address: ______________________

Phone Number: ______________________

Notes:

Neighbor:

Name: ______________________

Children: ______________________

____

Address: ______________________

Phone Number: ______________________

Notes:

HOME LIFE
Personal Finances

Bank: ______

Savings ☐ Checking ☐ Other: ______

Account #: ______ Routing #: ______

Customer Service #: ______

Lost or Stolen #: ______

Banker/Contact: ______

Website: ______

User ID: ______ Password: ______

Date changed: New Password: ______

Date changed: New Password: ______

Date changed: New Password: ______

Date changed: New Password: ______

Notes:

Bank: ______

Savings ☐ Checking ☐ Other: ______

Account #: ______ Routing #: ______

Customer Service #: ______

Lost or Stolen #: ______

Banker/Contact: ______

Website: ______

User ID: ______ Password: ______

Date changed: New Password: ______

Date changed: New Password: ______

Date changed: New Password: ______

Date changed: New Password: ______

Notes:

HOME LIFE
Personal Finances

Bank: ______

Savings ☐ Checking ☐ Other: ______

Account #: ______ Routing #: ______

Customer Service #: ______

Lost or Stolen #: ______

Banker/Contact: ______

Website: ______

User ID: ______ Password: ______

Date changed: New Password: ______

Date changed: New Password: ______

Date changed: New Password: ______

Date changed: New Password: ______

Notes:

Bank: ______

Savings ☐ Checking ☐ Other: ______

Account #: ______ Routing #: ______

Customer Service #: ______

Lost or Stolen #: ______

Banker/Contact: ______

Website: ______

User ID: ______ Password: ______

Date changed: New Password: ______

Date changed: New Password: ______

Date changed: New Password: ______

Date changed: New Password: ______

Notes:

HOME LIFE
Personal Finances

BANK: ____________________

SAVINGS ☐ CHECKING ☐ OTHER: ____________________

ACCOUNT #: ____________ ROUTING #: ____________

CUSTOMER SERVICE #: ____________________

LOST OR STOLEN #: ____________________

BANKER/CONTACT: ____________________

WEBSITE: ____________________

USER ID: ____________ PASSWORD: ____________

DATE CHANGED: NEW PASSWORD: ____________________

DATE CHANGED: NEW PASSWORD: ____________________

DATE CHANGED: NEW PASSWORD: ____________________

DATE CHANGED: NEW PASSWORD: ____________________

NOTES:

BANK: ____________________

SAVINGS ☐ CHECKING ☐ OTHER: ____________________

ACCOUNT #: ____________ ROUTING #: ____________

CUSTOMER SERVICE #: ____________________

LOST OR STOLEN #: ____________________

BANKER/CONTACT: ____________________

WEBSITE: ____________________

USER ID: ____________ PASSWORD: ____________

DATE CHANGED: NEW PASSWORD: ____________________

DATE CHANGED: NEW PASSWORD: ____________________

DATE CHANGED: NEW PASSWORD: ____________________

DATE CHANGED: NEW PASSWORD: ____________________

NOTES:

HOME LIFE
Personal Finances

BANK: ____

SAVINGS ☐ CHECKING ☐ OTHER: ____

ACCOUNT #: ____ ROUTING #: ____

CUSTOMER SERVICE #: ____

LOST OR STOLEN #: ____

BANKER/CONTACT: ____

WEBSITE: ____

USER ID: ____ PASSWORD: ____

DATE CHANGED: NEW PASSWORD: ____

DATE CHANGED: NEW PASSWORD: ____

DATE CHANGED: NEW PASSWORD: ____

DATE CHANGED: NEW PASSWORD: ____

NOTES:

BANK ACCOUNTS

BANK: ____

SAVINGS ☐ CHECKING ☐ OTHER: ____

ACCOUNT #: ____ ROUTING #: ____

CUSTOMER SERVICE #: ____

LOST OR STOLEN #: ____

BANKER/CONTACT: ____

WEBSITE: ____

USER ID: ____ PASSWORD: ____

DATE CHANGED: NEW PASSWORD: ____

DATE CHANGED: NEW PASSWORD: ____

DATE CHANGED: NEW PASSWORD: ____

DATE CHANGED: NEW PASSWORD: ____

NOTES:

HOME LIFE
Personal Finances

Bank: ____

Savings ☐ Checking ☐ Other: ______________

Account #: ______________ Routing #: ______________

Customer Service #: ______________________________

Lost or Stolen #: ______________________________

Banker/Contact: ______________________________

Website: ______________________________________

User ID: ______________ Password: ______________

Date changed: ______________ New Password: ______________

Date changed: ______________ New Password: ______________

Date changed: ______________ New Password: ______________

Date changed: ______________ New Password: ______________

Notes:

Bank: ____

Savings ☐ Checking ☐ Other: ______________

Account #: ______________ Routing #: ______________

Customer Service #: ______________________________

Lost or Stolen #: ______________________________

Banker/Contact: ______________________________

Website: ______________________________________

User ID: ______________ Password: ______________

Date changed: ______________ New Password: ______________

Date changed: ______________ New Password: ______________

Date changed: ______________ New Password: ______________

Date changed: ______________ New Password: ______________

Notes:

HOME LIFE
Personal Finances

Bank: ____________________

Savings ☐ Checking ☐ Other: ____________

Account #: ____________ Routing #: ____________

Customer Service #: ____________

Lost or Stolen #: ____________

Banker/Contact: ____________

Website: ____________

User ID: ____________ Password: ____________

Date changed: ____________ New Password: ____________

Date changed: ____________ New Password: ____________

Date changed: ____________ New Password: ____________

Date changed: ____________ New Password: ____________

Notes:

Bank: ____________________

Savings ☐ Checking ☐ Other: ____________

Account #: ____________ Routing #: ____________

Customer Service #: ____________

Lost or Stolen #: ____________

Banker/Contact: ____________

Website: ____________

User ID: ____________ Password: ____________

Date changed: ____________ New Password: ____________

Date changed: ____________ New Password: ____________

Date changed: ____________ New Password: ____________

Date changed: ____________ New Password: ____________

Notes:

Bank: ______

Savings ☐ Checking ☐ Other: ______

Account #: ______ Routing #: ______

Customer Service #: ______

Lost or Stolen #: ______

Banker/Contact: ______

Website: ______

User ID: ______ Password: ______

Date changed: ______ New Password: ______

Date changed: ______ New Password: ______

Date changed: ______ New Password: ______

Date changed: ______ New Password: ______

Notes:

Bank: ______

Savings ☐ Checking ☐ Other: ______

Account #: ______ Routing #: ______

Customer Service #: ______

Lost or Stolen #: ______

Banker/Contact: ______

Website: ______

User ID: ______ Password: ______

Date changed: ______ New Password: ______

Date changed: ______ New Password: ______

Date changed: ______ New Password: ______

Date changed: ______ New Password: ______

Notes:

Bank: ____________________

Savings ☐ Checking ☐ Other: ____________

Account #: ____________ Routing #: ____________

Customer Service #: ____________________

Lost or Stolen #: ____________________

Banker/Contact: ____________________

Website: ____________________

User ID: ____________ Password: ____________

Date changed: New Password: ____________

Date changed: New Password: ____________

Date changed: New Password: ____________

Date changed: New Password: ____________

Notes:

Bank: ____________________

Savings ☐ Checking ☐ Other: ____________

Account #: ____________ Routing #: ____________

Customer Service #: ____________________

Lost or Stolen #: ____________________

Banker/Contact: ____________________

Website: ____________________

User ID: ____________ Password: ____________

Date changed: New Password: ____________

Date changed: New Password: ____________

Date changed: New Password: ____________

Date changed: New Password: ____________

Notes:

HOME LIFE

Personal Finances

BANK: ____________________

SAVINGS ☐ CHECKING ☐ OTHER: ____________________

ACCOUNT #: ____________ ROUTING #: ____________

CUSTOMER SERVICE #: ____________________

LOST OR STOLEN #: ____________________

BANKER/CONTACT: ____________________

WEBSITE: ____________________

USER ID: ____________ PASSWORD: ____________

DATE CHANGED: NEW PASSWORD: ____________________

DATE CHANGED: NEW PASSWORD: ____________________

DATE CHANGED: NEW PASSWORD: ____________________

DATE CHANGED: NEW PASSWORD: ____________________

NOTES:

BANK: ____________________

SAVINGS ☐ CHECKING ☐ OTHER: ____________________

ACCOUNT #: ____________ ROUTING #: ____________

CUSTOMER SERVICE #: ____________________

LOST OR STOLEN #: ____________________

BANKER/CONTACT: ____________________

WEBSITE: ____________________

USER ID: ____________ PASSWORD: ____________

DATE CHANGED: NEW PASSWORD: ____________________

DATE CHANGED: NEW PASSWORD: ____________________

DATE CHANGED: NEW PASSWORD: ____________________

DATE CHANGED: NEW PASSWORD: ____________________

NOTES:

HOME LIFE

Personal Finances

Bank: ____________________

Savings ☐ Checking ☐ Other: ____________

Account #: ____________ Routing #: ____________

Customer Service #: ____________________

Lost or Stolen #: ____________________

Banker/Contact: ____________________

Website: ____________________

User ID: ____________ Password: ____________

Date changed: New Password: ____________

Date changed: New Password: ____________

Date changed: New Password: ____________

Date changed: New Password: ____________

Notes:

Bank: ____________________

Savings ☐ Checking ☐ Other: ____________

Account #: ____________ Routing #: ____________

Customer Service #: ____________________

Lost or Stolen #: ____________________

Banker/Contact: ____________________

Website: ____________________

User ID: ____________ Password: ____________

Date changed: New Password: ____________

Date changed: New Password: ____________

Date changed: New Password: ____________

Date changed: New Password: ____________

Notes:

Personal Finances

Bank: ____________________

Home ☐ Auto ☐ Credit Card ☐ Other: __________

Associated collateral: ____________________

Account #: ____________________

Customer Service #: ____________________

Lost or Stolen #: ____________________

Date Opened: / / Revolving ☐

Date scheduled to finish: / /

Interest Rate: ______ %

Minimum Payment: $ ______

Website: ____________________

User ID: __________ Password: __________

Notes:

Bank: ____________________

Home ☐ Auto ☐ Credit Card ☐ Other: __________

Associated collateral: ____________________

Account #: ____________________

Customer Service #: ____________________

Lost or Stolen #: ____________________

Date Opened: / / Revolving ☐

Date scheduled to finish: / /

Interest Rate: ______ %

Minimum Payment: $ ______

Website: ____________________

User ID: __________ Password: __________

Notes:

HOME LIFE

Personal Finances

BANK: ______________________

HOME ☐ AUTO ☐ CREDIT CARD ☐ OTHER: __________

ASSOCIATED COLLATERAL: ______________________

ACCOUNT #: ______________________

CUSTOMER SERVICE #: ______________________

LOST OR STOLEN #: ______________________

DATE OPENED: / / REVOLVING ☐

DATE SCHEDULED TO FINISH: / /

INTEREST RATE: ________ %

MINIMUM PAYMENT: $__________

WEBSITE: ______________________

USER ID: ______________ PASSWORD: ______________

NOTES:

BANK: ______________________

HOME ☐ AUTO ☐ CREDIT CARD ☐ OTHER: __________

ASSOCIATED COLLATERAL: ______________________

ACCOUNT #: ______________________

CUSTOMER SERVICE #: ______________________

LOST OR STOLEN #: ______________________

DATE OPENED: / / REVOLVING ☐

DATE SCHEDULED TO FINISH: / /

INTEREST RATE: ________ %

MINIMUM PAYMENT: $__________

WEBSITE: ______________________

USER ID: ______________ PASSWORD: ______________

NOTES:

HOME LIFE

Personal Finances

Bank: ____________________

Home ☐ Auto ☐ Credit Card ☐ Other: __________

Associated collateral: ____________________

Account #: ____________________

Customer Service #: ____________________

Lost or Stolen #: ____________________

Date Opened: / / Revolving ☐

Date scheduled to finish: / /

Interest Rate: ________%

Minimum Payment: $__________

Website: ____________________

User ID: __________ Password: __________

Notes:

Bank: ____________________

Home ☐ Auto ☐ Credit Card ☐ Other: __________

Associated collateral: ____________________

Account #: ____________________

Customer Service #: ____________________

Lost or Stolen #: ____________________

Date Opened: / / Revolving ☐

Date scheduled to finish: / /

Interest Rate: ________%

Minimum Payment: $__________

Website: ____________________

User ID: __________ Password: __________

Notes:

HOME LIFE

Personal Finances

Bank: ____________________

Home ☐ Auto ☐ Credit Card ☐ Other: __________

Associated collateral: ____________________

Account #: ____________________

Customer Service #: ____________________

Lost or Stolen #: ____________________

Date Opened: / / Revolving ☐

Date scheduled to finish: / /

Interest Rate: ________ %

Minimum Payment: $__________

Website: ____________________

User ID: __________ Password: __________

Notes:

Bank: ____________________

Home ☐ Auto ☐ Credit Card ☐ Other: __________

Associated collateral: ____________________

Account #: ____________________

Customer Service #: ____________________

Lost or Stolen #: ____________________

Date Opened: / / Revolving ☐

Date scheduled to finish: / /

Interest Rate: ________ %

Minimum Payment: $__________

Website: ____________________

User ID: __________ Password: __________

Notes:

Personal Finances

Bank: ____________________

Home ☐ Auto ☐ Credit Card ☐ Other: ____________

Associated collateral: ____________________

Account #: ____________________

Customer Service #: ____________________

Lost or Stolen #: ____________________

Date Opened: / / Revolving ☐

Date scheduled to finish: / /

Interest Rate: ________ %

Minimum Payment: $ ____________

Website: ____________________

User ID: ____________ Password: ____________

Notes:

Bank: ____________________

Home ☐ Auto ☐ Credit Card ☐ Other: ____________

Associated collateral: ____________________

Account #: ____________________

Customer Service #: ____________________

Lost or Stolen #: ____________________

Date Opened: / / Revolving ☐

Date scheduled to finish: / /

Interest Rate: ________ %

Minimum Payment: $ ____________

Website: ____________________

User ID: ____________ Password: ____________

Notes:

HOME LIFE
Personal Finances

Bank: ____________________

Home ☐ Auto ☐ Credit Card ☐ Other: __________

Associated collateral: ____________________

Account #: ____________________

Customer Service #: ____________________

Lost or Stolen #: ____________________

Date Opened: / / Revolving ☐

Date scheduled to finish: / /

Interest Rate: ________ %

Minimum Payment: $__________

Website: ____________________

User ID: __________ Password: __________

Notes:

Bank: ____________________

Home ☐ Auto ☐ Credit Card ☐ Other: __________

Associated collateral: ____________________

Account #: ____________________

Customer Service #: ____________________

Lost or Stolen #: ____________________

Date Opened: / / Revolving ☐

Date scheduled to finish: / /

Interest Rate: ________ %

Minimum Payment: $__________

Website: ____________________

User ID: __________ Password: __________

Notes:

Bank: ____________________

Home ☐ Auto ☐ Credit Card ☐ Other: ____________

Associated collateral: ____________________

Account #: ____________________

Customer Service #: ____________________

Lost or Stolen #: ____________________

Date Opened: / / Revolving ☐

Date scheduled to finish: / /

Interest Rate: ________ %

Minimum Payment: $ ____________

Website: ____________________

User ID: ____________ Password: ____________

Notes:

Bank: ____________________

Home ☐ Auto ☐ Credit Card ☐ Other: ____________

Associated collateral: ____________________

Account #: ____________________

Customer Service #: ____________________

Lost or Stolen #: ____________________

Date Opened: / / Revolving ☐

Date scheduled to finish: / /

Interest Rate: ________ %

Minimum Payment: $ ____________

Website: ____________________

User ID: ____________ Password: ____________

Notes:

HOME LIFE

Personal Finances

Bank: ______________________________
Home ☐ Auto ☐ Credit Card ☐ Other: __________
Associated collateral: ______________________
Account #: ______________________________
Customer Service #: ______________________
Lost or Stolen #: ______________________
Date Opened: / / Revolving ☐
Date scheduled to finish: / /
Interest Rate: ________ %
Minimum Payment: $ __________
Website: ______________________________
User ID: ______________ Password: ______________
Notes:

Bank: ______________________________
Home ☐ Auto ☐ Credit Card ☐ Other: __________
Associated collateral: ______________________
Account #: ______________________________
Customer Service #: ______________________
Lost or Stolen #: ______________________
Date Opened: / / Revolving ☐
Date scheduled to finish: / /
Interest Rate: ________ %
Minimum Payment: $ __________
Website: ______________________________
User ID: ______________ Password: ______________
Notes:

HOME LIFE

Personal Finances

Bank: ______

Home ☐ Auto ☐ Credit Card ☐ Other: ______

Associated collateral: ______

Account #: ______

Customer Service #: ______

Lost or Stolen #: ______

Date Opened: / / Revolving ☐

Date scheduled to finish: / /

Interest Rate: ______%

Minimum Payment: $______

Website: ______

User ID: ______ Password: ______

Notes:

Bank: ______

Home ☐ Auto ☐ Credit Card ☐ Other: ______

Associated collateral: ______

Account #: ______

Customer Service #: ______

Lost or Stolen #: ______

Date Opened: / / Revolving ☐

Date scheduled to finish: / /

Interest Rate: ______%

Minimum Payment: $______

Website: ______

User ID: ______ Password: ______

Notes:

BANK: ______

HOME ☐ AUTO ☐ CREDIT CARD ☐ OTHER: ______

ASSOCIATED COLLATERAL: ______

ACCOUNT #: ______

CUSTOMER SERVICE #: ______

LOST OR STOLEN #: ______

DATE OPENED: / / REVOLVING ☐

DATE SCHEDULED TO FINISH: / /

INTEREST RATE: ______ %

MINIMUM PAYMENT: $ ______

WEBSITE: ______

USER ID: ______ PASSWORD: ______

NOTES:

BANK: ______

HOME ☐ AUTO ☐ CREDIT CARD ☐ OTHER: ______

ASSOCIATED COLLATERAL: ______

ACCOUNT #: ______

CUSTOMER SERVICE #: ______

LOST OR STOLEN #: ______

DATE OPENED: / / REVOLVING ☐

DATE SCHEDULED TO FINISH: / /

INTEREST RATE: ______ %

MINIMUM PAYMENT: $ ______

WEBSITE: ______

USER ID: ______ PASSWORD: ______

NOTES:

HOME LIFE

Subscriptions

Company: ______________________________

Yearly ☐ Monthly ☐ Weekly ☐ Other: __________

Service: ______________________________

Account #: ______________________________

Customer Service #: ______________________________

Website: ______________________________

Date Opened: / / Auto-Renew ☐

Date scheduled to finish: / /

Business Related ☐ Deductible ☐ Reimbursable ☐

Recurring Payment: $ __________

User ID: ______________ Password: ______________

Associated Email: ______________________________

Notes:

Company: ______________________________

Yearly ☐ Monthly ☐ Weekly ☐ Other: __________

Service: ______________________________

Account #: ______________________________

Customer Service #: ______________________________

Website: ______________________________

Date Opened: / / Auto-Renew ☐

Date scheduled to finish: / /

Business Related ☐ Deductible ☐ Reimbursable ☐

Recurring Payment: $ __________

User ID: ______________ Password: ______________

Associated Email: ______________________________

Notes:

HOME LIFE
Subscriptions

Company: ____________________
Yearly ☐ Monthly ☐ Weekly ☐ Other: ________
Service: ____________________
Account #: ____________________
Customer Service #: ____________________
Website: ____________________
Date Opened: / / Auto-Renew ☐
Date scheduled to finish: / /
Business Related ☐ Deductible ☐ Reimbursable ☐
Recurring Payment: $ ________
User ID: ________ Password: ________
Associated Email: ____________________
Notes:

Company: ____________________
Yearly ☐ Monthly ☐ Weekly ☐ Other: ________
Service: ____________________
Account #: ____________________
Customer Service #: ____________________
Website: ____________________
Date Opened: / / Auto-Renew ☐
Date scheduled to finish: / /
Business Related ☐ Deductible ☐ Reimbursable ☐
Recurring Payment: $ ________
User ID: ________ Password: ________
Associated Email: ____________________
Notes:

HOME LIFE

Subscriptions

Company: ____________________

Yearly ☐ Monthly ☐ Weekly ☐ Other: ____________

Service: ____________________

Account #: ____________________

Customer Service #: ____________________

Website: ____________________

Date Opened: / / Auto-Renew ☐

Date scheduled to finish: / /

Business Related ☐ Deductible ☐ Reimbursable ☐

Recurring Payment: $ ____________

User ID: ____________ Password: ____________

Associated Email: ____________________

Notes:

Company: ____________________

Yearly ☐ Monthly ☐ Weekly ☐ Other: ____________

Service: ____________________

Account #: ____________________

Customer Service #: ____________________

Website: ____________________

Date Opened: / / Auto-Renew ☐

Date scheduled to finish: / /

Business Related ☐ Deductible ☐ Reimbursable ☐

Recurring Payment: $ ____________

User ID: ____________ Password: ____________

Associated Email: ____________________

Notes:

HOME LIFE
Subscriptions

COMPANY: ______________________________

YEARLY ☐ MONTHLY ☐ WEEKLY ☐ OTHER: __________

SERVICE: ______________________________

ACCOUNT #: ______________________________

CUSTOMER SERVICE #: ______________________________

WEBSITE: ______________________________

DATE OPENED: / / AUTO-RENEW ☐

DATE SCHEDULED TO FINISH: / /

BUSINESS RELATED ☐ DEDUCTIBLE ☐ REIMBURSABLE ☐

RECURRING PAYMENT: $ __________

USER ID: __________ PASSWORD: __________

ASSOCIATED EMAIL: ______________________________

NOTES:

COMPANY: ______________________________

YEARLY ☐ MONTHLY ☐ WEEKLY ☐ OTHER: __________

SERVICE: ______________________________

ACCOUNT #: ______________________________

CUSTOMER SERVICE #: ______________________________

WEBSITE: ______________________________

DATE OPENED: / / AUTO-RENEW ☐

DATE SCHEDULED TO FINISH: / /

BUSINESS RELATED ☐ DEDUCTIBLE ☐ REIMBURSABLE ☐

RECURRING PAYMENT: $ __________

USER ID: __________ PASSWORD: __________

ASSOCIATED EMAIL: ______________________________

NOTES:

HOME LIFE
Subscriptions

Company: ______

Yearly ☐ Monthly ☐ Weekly ☐ Other: ______

Service: ______

Account #: ______

Customer Service #: ______

Website: ______

Date Opened: / / Auto-Renew ☐

Date scheduled to finish: / /

Business Related ☐ Deductible ☐ Reimbursable ☐

Recurring Payment: $ ______

User ID: ______ Password: ______

Associated Email: ______

Notes:

Company: ______

Yearly ☐ Monthly ☐ Weekly ☐ Other: ______

Service: ______

Account #: ______

Customer Service #: ______

Website: ______

Date Opened: / / Auto-Renew ☐

Date scheduled to finish: / /

Business Related ☐ Deductible ☐ Reimbursable ☐

Recurring Payment: $ ______

User ID: ______ Password: ______

Associated Email: ______

Notes:

HOME LIFE
Subscriptions

SUBSCRIPTIONS

Company:
Yearly ☐ Monthly ☐ Weekly ☐ Other:
Service:
Account #:
Customer Service #:
Website:
Date Opened: / / Auto-Renew ☐
Date scheduled to finish: / /
Business Related ☐ Deductible ☐ Reimbursable ☐
Recurring Payment: $
User ID: Password:
Associated Email:
Notes:

Company:
Yearly ☐ Monthly ☐ Weekly ☐ Other:
Service:
Account #:
Customer Service #:
Website:
Date Opened: / / Auto-Renew ☐
Date scheduled to finish: / /
Business Related ☐ Deductible ☐ Reimbursable ☐
Recurring Payment: $
User ID: Password:
Associated Email:
Notes:

HOME LIFE
Subscriptions

Company: ____________________

Yearly ☐ Monthly ☐ Weekly ☐ Other: ________

Service: ____________________

Account #: ____________________

Customer Service #: ____________________

Website: ____________________

Date Opened: / / Auto-Renew ☐

Date scheduled to finish: / /

Business Related ☐ Deductible ☐ Reimbursable ☐

Recurring Payment: $ ________

User ID: ________ Password: ________

Associated Email: ____________________

Notes:

Company: ____________________

Yearly ☐ Monthly ☐ Weekly ☐ Other: ________

Service: ____________________

Account #: ____________________

Customer Service #: ____________________

Website: ____________________

Date Opened: / / Auto-Renew ☐

Date scheduled to finish: / /

Business Related ☐ Deductible ☐ Reimbursable ☐

Recurring Payment: $ ________

User ID: ________ Password: ________

Associated Email: ____________________

Notes:

HOME LIFE
Subscriptions

Company: ______________________

Yearly ☐ Monthly ☐ Weekly ☐ Other: __________

Service: ______________________

Account #: ______________________

Customer Service #: ______________________

Website: ______________________

Date Opened: / / Auto-Renew ☐

Date scheduled to finish: / /

Business Related ☐ Deductible ☐ Reimbursable ☐

Recurring Payment: $ __________

User ID: __________ Password: __________

Associated Email: ______________________

Notes:

Company: ______________________

Yearly ☐ Monthly ☐ Weekly ☐ Other: __________

Service: ______________________

Account #: ______________________

Customer Service #: ______________________

Website: ______________________

Date Opened: / / Auto-Renew ☐

Date scheduled to finish: / /

Business Related ☐ Deductible ☐ Reimbursable ☐

Recurring Payment: $ __________

User ID: __________ Password: __________

Associated Email: ______________________

Notes:

HOME LIFE
Subscriptions

Company:
Yearly ☐ Monthly ☐ Weekly ☐ Other:
Service:
Account #:
Customer Service #:
Website:
Date Opened: / / Auto-Renew ☐
Date scheduled to finish: / /
Business Related ☐ Deductible ☐ Reimbursable ☐
Recurring Payment: $
User ID: Password:
Associated Email:
Notes:

Company:
Yearly ☐ Monthly ☐ Weekly ☐ Other:
Service:
Account #:
Customer Service #:
Website:
Date Opened: / / Auto-Renew ☐
Date scheduled to finish: / /
Business Related ☐ Deductible ☐ Reimbursable ☐
Recurring Payment: $
User ID: Password:
Associated Email:
Notes:

HOME LIFE
Subscriptions

SUBSCRIPTIONS

Company: ____________________

Yearly ☐ Monthly ☐ Weekly ☐ Other: __________

Service: ____________________

Account #: ____________________

Customer Service #: ____________________

Website: ____________________

Date Opened: / / Auto-Renew ☐

Date scheduled to finish: / /

Business Related ☐ Deductible ☐ Reimbursable ☐

Recurring Payment: $ __________

User ID: __________ Password: __________

Associated Email: ____________________

Notes:

Company: ____________________

Yearly ☐ Monthly ☐ Weekly ☐ Other: __________

Service: ____________________

Account #: ____________________

Customer Service #: ____________________

Website: ____________________

Date Opened: / / Auto-Renew ☐

Date scheduled to finish: / /

Business Related ☐ Deductible ☐ Reimbursable ☐

Recurring Payment: $ __________

User ID: __________ Password: __________

Associated Email: ____________________

Notes:

HOME LIFE

Insurance/Utilities/Inventory

Provider: ____________________

Life ☐ Home Owner/Renter ☐ Auto ☐ Other: ____________________

Policy #: ____________________

Deductible: ____________________

Coverage: ____________________

____

____

Premium: $ __________ Every: Month ☐ Year ☐

Agent: ____________________

Phone #: ____________________

Email: ____________________

Website: ____________________

Notes: ____________________

Provider: ____________________

Life ☐ Home Owner/Renter ☐ Auto ☐ Other: ____________________

Policy #: ____________________

Deductible: ____________________

Coverage: ____________________

____

____

Premium: $ __________ Every: Month ☐ Year ☐

Agent: ____________________

Phone #: ____________________

Email: ____________________

Website: ____________________

Notes: ____________________

HOME LIFE

Insurance/Utilities/Inventory

PROVIDER: ______________________

LIFE ☐ HOME OWNER/RENTER ☐ AUTO ☐ OTHER: __________

POLICY #: ______________________

DEDUCTIBLE: ______________________

COVERAGE: ______________________

PREMIUM: $ __________ EVERY: MONTH ☐ YEAR ☐

AGENT: ______________________

PHONE #: ______________________

EMAIL: ______________________

WEBSITE: ______________________

NOTES:

PROVIDER: ______________________

LIFE ☐ HOME OWNER/RENTER ☐ AUTO ☐ OTHER: __________

POLICY #: ______________________

DEDUCTIBLE: ______________________

COVERAGE: ______________________

PREMIUM: $ __________ EVERY: MONTH ☐ YEAR ☐

AGENT: ______________________

PHONE #: ______________________

EMAIL: ______________________

WEBSITE: ______________________

NOTES:

HOME LIFE
Insurance/Utilities/Inventory

PROVIDER: ______
SERVICE: ______
ACCOUNT #: ______
WEBSITE: ______
USER ID: ______ PASSWORD: ______
CUSTOMER SERVICE: ______
EMAIL: ______
NOTES:

PROVIDER: ______
SERVICE: ______
ACCOUNT #: ______
WEBSITE: ______
USER ID: ______ PASSWORD: ______
CUSTOMER SERVICE: ______
EMAIL: ______
NOTES:

PROVIDER: ______
SERVICE: ______
ACCOUNT #: ______
WEBSITE: ______
USER ID: ______ PASSWORD: ______
CUSTOMER SERVICE: ______
EMAIL: ______
NOTES:

HOME LIFE

Insurance/Utilities/Inventory

Provider: ______________________________
Service: ______________________________
Account #: ______________________________
Website: ______________________________
User ID: ______________ Password: ______________
Customer Service: ______________________________
Email: ______________________________
Notes:

Provider: ______________________________
Service: ______________________________
Account #: ______________________________
Website: ______________________________
User ID: ______________ Password: ______________
Customer Service: ______________________________
Email: ______________________________
Notes:

Provider: ______________________________
Service: ______________________________
Account #: ______________________________
Website: ______________________________
User ID: ______________ Password: ______________
Customer Service: ______________________________
Email: ______________________________
Notes:

HOME LIFE

Insurance/Utilities/Inventory

Provider:
Service:
Account #:
Website:
User ID: Password:
Customer Service:
Email:
Notes:

Provider:
Service:
Account #:
Website:
User ID: Password:
Customer Service:
Email:
Notes:

Provider:
Service:
Account #:
Website:
User ID: Password:
Customer Service:
Email:
Notes:

HOME LIFE

Insurance/Utilities/Inventory

Provider: ____________________
Service: ____________________
Account #: ____________________
Website: ____________________
User ID: __________ Password: __________
Customer Service: ____________________
Email: ____________________
Notes:

Provider: ____________________
Service: ____________________
Account #: ____________________
Website: ____________________
User ID: __________ Password: __________
Customer Service: ____________________
Email: ____________________
Notes:

UTILITIES

Provider: ____________________
Service: ____________________
Account #: ____________________
Website: ____________________
User ID: __________ Password: __________
Customer Service: ____________________
Email: ____________________
Notes:

HOME LIFE

Insurance/Utilities/Inventory

Provider: ____________________
Service: ____________________
Account #: ____________________
Website: ____________________
User ID: __________ Password: __________
Customer Service: ____________________
Email: ____________________
Notes:

Provider: ____________________
Service: ____________________
Account #: ____________________
Website: ____________________
User ID: __________ Password: __________
Customer Service: ____________________
Email: ____________________
Notes:

Provider: ____________________
Service: ____________________
Account #: ____________________
Website: ____________________
User ID: __________ Password: __________
Customer Service: ____________________
Email: ____________________
Notes:

HOME LIFE

Insurance/Utilities/Inventory

Provider: ______________________________

Service: ______________________________

Account #: ______________________________

Website: ______________________________

User ID: ______________ Password: ______________

Customer Service: ______________________________

Email: ______________________________

Notes:

Provider: ______________________________

Service: ______________________________

Account #: ______________________________

Website: ______________________________

User ID: ______________ Password: ______________

Customer Service: ______________________________

Email: ______________________________

Notes:

Provider: ______________________________

Service: ______________________________

Account #: ______________________________

Website: ______________________________

User ID: ______________ Password: ______________

Customer Service: ______________________________

Email: ______________________________

Notes:

HOME LIFE

Insurance/Utilities/Inventory

Provider: ______________________

Service: ______________________

Account #: ______________________

Website: ______________________

User ID: ____________ Password: ____________

Customer Service: ______________________

Email: ______________________

Notes:

Provider: ______________________

Service: ______________________

Account #: ______________________

Website: ______________________

User ID: ____________ Password: ____________

Customer Service: ______________________

Email: ______________________

Notes:

Provider: ______________________

Service: ______________________

Account #: ______________________

Website: ______________________

User ID: ____________ Password: ____________

Customer Service: ______________________

Email: ______________________

Notes:

HOME LIFE

Insurance/Utilities/Inventory

Provider: ____________________

Service: ____________________

Account #: ____________________

Website: ____________________

User ID: __________ Password: __________

Customer Service: ____________________

Email: ____________________

Notes:

Provider: ____________________

Service: ____________________

Account #: ____________________

Website: ____________________

User ID: __________ Password: __________

Customer Service: ____________________

Email: ____________________

Notes:

Provider: ____________________

Service: ____________________

Account #: ____________________

Website: ____________________

User ID: __________ Password: __________

Customer Service: ____________________

Email: ____________________

Notes:

HOME LIFE

Insurance/Utilities/Inventory

Provider: ______________________________
Service: ______________________________
Account #: ______________________________
Website: ______________________________
User ID: ______________ Password: ______________
Customer Service: ______________________________
Email: ______________________________
Notes:

Provider: ______________________________
Service: ______________________________
Account #: ______________________________
Website: ______________________________
User ID: ______________ Password: ______________
Customer Service: ______________________________
Email: ______________________________
Notes:

Provider: ______________________________
Service: ______________________________
Account #: ______________________________
Website: ______________________________
User ID: ______________ Password: ______________
Customer Service: ______________________________
Email: ______________________________
Notes:

HOME LIFE
Insurance/Utilities/Inventory

PROVIDER: ______________________________
SERVICE: ______________________________
ACCOUNT #: ______________________________
WEBSITE: ______________________________
USER ID: ______________ PASSWORD: ______________
CUSTOMER SERVICE: ______________________________
EMAIL: ______________________________
NOTES:

PROVIDER: ______________________________
SERVICE: ______________________________
ACCOUNT #: ______________________________
WEBSITE: ______________________________
USER ID: ______________ PASSWORD: ______________
CUSTOMER SERVICE: ______________________________
EMAIL: ______________________________
NOTES:

PROVIDER: ______________________________
SERVICE: ______________________________
ACCOUNT #: ______________________________
WEBSITE: ______________________________
USER ID: ______________ PASSWORD: ______________
CUSTOMER SERVICE: ______________________________
EMAIL: ______________________________
NOTES:

HOME LIFE

Insurance/Utilities/Inventory

Item Description:
Brand: Model:
Date Purchased:
Amount Paid: $ Form of payment:
Identifying numbers:
Registered: Yes No NA
Customer Service:
Email:
Website:
User ID: Password:
Warranty:
Extended Warr. Purchased:
Warranty Phone #:
Notes:

Item Description:
Brand: Model:
Date Purchased:
Amount Paid: $ Form of payment:
Identifying numbers:
Registered: Yes No NA
Customer Service:
Email:
Website:
User ID: Password:
Warranty:
Extended Warr. Purchased:
Warranty Phone #:
Notes:

Item Description:____________________

Brand:____________ Model:____________

Date Purchased:____________________

Amount Paid: $ ____________ Form of payment:____________

Identifying numbers:____________________

Registered: Yes No NA

Customer Service:____________________

Email:____________________

Website:____________________

User ID:____________ Password:____________

Warranty:____________________

Extended Warr. Purchased:____________________

Warranty Phone #:____________________

Notes:

Item Description:____________________

Brand:____________ Model:____________

Date Purchased:____________________

Amount Paid: $ ____________ Form of payment:____________

Identifying numbers:____________________

Registered: Yes No NA

Customer Service:____________________

Email:____________________

Website:____________________

User ID:____________ Password:____________

Warranty:____________________

Extended Warr. Purchased:____________________

Warranty Phone #:____________________

Notes:

HOME LIFE

Insurance/Utilities/Inventory

Item Description: ______

Brand: ______ Model: ______

Date Purchased: ______

Amount Paid: $ ______ Form of payment: ______

Identifying numbers: ______

Registered: Yes No NA

Customer Service: ______

Email: ______

Website: ______

User ID: ______ Password: ______

Warranty: ______

Extended Warr. Purchased: ______

Warranty Phone #: ______

Notes:

Item Description: ______

Brand: ______ Model: ______

Date Purchased: ______

Amount Paid: $ ______ Form of payment: ______

Identifying numbers: ______

Registered: Yes No NA

Customer Service: ______

Email: ______

Website: ______

User ID: ______ Password: ______

Warranty: ______

Extended Warr. Purchased: ______

Warranty Phone #: ______

Notes:

HOME LIFE

Insurance/Utilities/Inventory

Item Description: ____________________

Brand: ____________ Model: ____________

Date Purchased: ____________________

Amount Paid: $ ____________ Form of payment: ____________

Identifying numbers: ____________________

Registered: Yes No NA

Customer Service: ____________________

Email: ____________________

Website: ____________________

User ID: ____________ Password: ____________

Warranty: ____________________

Extended Warr. Purchased: ____________________

Warranty Phone #: ____________________

Notes:

Item Description: ____________________

Brand: ____________ Model: ____________

Date Purchased: ____________________

Amount Paid: $ ____________ Form of payment: ____________

Identifying numbers: ____________________

Registered: Yes No NA

Customer Service: ____________________

Email: ____________________

Website: ____________________

User ID: ____________ Password: ____________

Warranty: ____________________

Extended Warr. Purchased: ____________________

Warranty Phone #: ____________________

Notes:

HOME LIFE

Insurance/Utilities/Inventory

Item Description: ______

Brand: ______ Model: ______

Date Purchased: ______

Amount Paid: $ ______ Form of payment: ______

Identifying numbers: ______

Registered: Yes No NA

Customer Service: ______

Email: ______

Website: ______

User ID: ______ Password: ______

Warranty: ______

Extended Warr. Purchased: ______

Warranty Phone #: ______

Notes:

Item Description: ______

Brand: ______ Model: ______

Date Purchased: ______

Amount Paid: $ ______ Form of payment: ______

Identifying numbers: ______

Registered: Yes No NA

Customer Service: ______

Email: ______

Website: ______

User ID: ______ Password: ______

Warranty: ______

Extended Warr. Purchased: ______

Warranty Phone #: ______

Notes:

HOME LIFE

Insurance/Utilities/Inventory

Item Description: ____
Brand: ______________________ Model: ________________________
Date Purchased: ____
Amount Paid: $ ________________ Form of payment: ______________
Identifying numbers: ______________________________________
Registered: Yes No NA
Customer Service: ____
Email: ____
Website: ____
User ID: ________________ Password: __________________________
Warranty: ____
Extended Warr. Purchased: ___________________________________
Warranty Phone #: ____
Notes:

Item Description: ____
Brand: ______________________ Model: ________________________
Date Purchased: ____
Amount Paid: $ ________________ Form of payment: ______________
Identifying numbers: ______________________________________
Registered: Yes No NA
Customer Service: ____
Email: ____
Website: ____
User ID: ________________ Password: __________________________
Warranty: ____
Extended Warr. Purchased: ___________________________________
Warranty Phone #: ____
Notes:

HOME LIFE

Insurance/Utilities/Inventory

Item Description: ____________________

Brand: ____________ Model: ____________

Date Purchased: ____________________

Amount Paid: $ ____________ Form of payment: ____________

Identifying numbers: ____________________

Registered: Yes No NA

Customer Service: ____________________

Email: ____________________

Website: ____________________

User ID: ____________ Password: ____________

Warranty: ____________________

Extended Warr. Purchased: ____________________

Warranty Phone #: ____________________

Notes:

Item Description: ____________________

Brand: ____________ Model: ____________

Date Purchased: ____________________

Amount Paid: $ ____________ Form of payment: ____________

Identifying numbers: ____________________

Registered: Yes No NA

Customer Service: ____________________

Email: ____________________

Website: ____________________

User ID: ____________ Password: ____________

Warranty: ____________________

Extended Warr. Purchased: ____________________

Warranty Phone #: ____________________

Notes:

HOME LIFE

Insurance/Utilities/Inventory

ITEM DESCRIPTION:

BRAND: MODEL:

DATE PURCHASED:

AMOUNT PAID: $ FORM OF PAYMENT:

IDENTIFYING NUMBERS:

REGISTERED: YES NO NA

CUSTOMER SERVICE:

EMAIL:

WEBSITE:

USER ID: PASSWORD:

WARRANTY:

EXTENDED WARR. PURCHASED:

WARRANTY PHONE #:

NOTES:

ITEM DESCRIPTION:

BRAND: MODEL:

DATE PURCHASED:

AMOUNT PAID: $ FORM OF PAYMENT:

IDENTIFYING NUMBERS:

REGISTERED: YES NO NA

CUSTOMER SERVICE:

EMAIL:

WEBSITE:

USER ID: PASSWORD:

WARRANTY:

EXTENDED WARR. PURCHASED:

WARRANTY PHONE #:

NOTES:

HOME LIFE

Insurance/Utilities/Inventory

Item Description:__________________________________

Brand:__________________ Model:__________________

Date Purchased:__________________________________

Amount Paid: $______________ Form of payment:____________

Identifying numbers:__________________________________

Registered: Yes No NA

Customer Service:__________________________________

Email:__________________________________

Website:__________________________________

User ID:______________ Password:__________________

Warranty:__________________________________

Extended Warr. Purchased:____________________________

Warranty Phone #:__________________________________

Notes:

Item Description:__________________________________

Brand:__________________ Model:__________________

Date Purchased:__________________________________

Amount Paid: $______________ Form of payment:____________

Identifying numbers:__________________________________

Registered: Yes No NA

Customer Service:__________________________________

Email:__________________________________

Website:__________________________________

User ID:______________ Password:__________________

Warranty:__________________________________

Extended Warr. Purchased:____________________________

Warranty Phone #:__________________________________

Notes:

HOME LIFE

Insurance/Utilities/Inventory

Item Description:

Brand: Model:

Date Purchased:

Amount Paid: $ Form of payment:

Identifying numbers:

Registered: Yes No NA

Customer Service:

Email:

Website:

User ID: Password:

Warranty:

Extended Warr. Purchased:

Warranty Phone #:

Notes:

Item Description:

Brand: Model:

Date Purchased:

Amount Paid: $ Form of payment:

Identifying numbers:

Registered: Yes No NA

Customer Service:

Email:

Website:

User ID: Password:

Warranty:

Extended Warr. Purchased:

Warranty Phone #:

Notes:

HOME LIFE

Insurance/Utilities/Inventory

Item Description:
Brand: Model:
Date Purchased:
Amount Paid: $ Form of payment:
Identifying numbers:
Registered: Yes No NA
Customer Service:
Email:
Website:
User ID: Password:
Warranty:
Extended Warr. Purchased:
Warranty Phone #:
Notes:

Item Description:
Brand: Model:
Date Purchased:
Amount Paid: $ Form of payment:
Identifying numbers:
Registered: Yes No NA
Customer Service:
Email:
Website:
User ID: Password:
Warranty:
Extended Warr. Purchased:
Warranty Phone #:
Notes:

HOME LIFE

Insurance/Utilities/Inventory

Item Description: ______

Brand: ______ Model: ______

Date Purchased: ______

Amount Paid: $ ______ Form of payment: ______

Identifying numbers: ______

Registered: Yes No NA

Customer Service: ______

Email: ______

Website: ______

User ID: ______ Password: ______

Warranty: ______

Extended Warr. Purchased: ______

Warranty Phone #: ______

Notes:

Item Description: ______

Brand: ______ Model: ______

Date Purchased: ______

Amount Paid: $ ______ Form of payment: ______

Identifying numbers: ______

Registered: Yes No NA

Customer Service: ______

Email: ______

Website: ______

User ID: ______ Password: ______

Warranty: ______

Extended Warr. Purchased: ______

Warranty Phone #: ______

Notes:

HOME LIFE

Service Providers

Service: __________
Provider Name: __________
Company Name: __________
Address: __________ Unit: _____
City: __________ State: _____ Zip: _____
Phone Number: __________
Email: __________
Website: __________
User ID: __________ Password: __________
Notes:

Service: __________
Provider Name: __________
Company Name: __________
Address: __________ Unit: _____
City: __________ State: _____ Zip: _____
Phone Number: __________
Email: __________
Website: __________
User ID: __________ Password: __________
Notes:

Service: __________
Provider Name: __________
Company Name: __________
Address: __________ Unit: _____
City: __________ State: _____ Zip: _____
Phone Number: __________
Email: __________
Website: __________
User ID: __________ Password: __________
Notes:

HOME LIFE
Service Providers

Service:
Provider Name:
Company Name:
Address: Unit:
City: State: Zip:
Phone Number:
Email:
Website:
User ID: Password:
Notes:

Service:
Provider Name:
Company Name:
Address: Unit:
City: State: Zip:
Phone Number:
Email:
Website:
User ID: Password:
Notes:

Service:
Provider Name:
Company Name:
Address: Unit:
City: State: Zip:
Phone Number:
Email:
Website:
User ID: Password:
Notes:

HOME LIFE

Service Providers

Service: ______________________________
Provider Name: ______________________________
Company Name: ______________________________
Address: ______________________ Unit: __________
City: ______________ State: __________ Zip: __________
Phone Number: ______________________________
Email: ______________________________
Website: ______________________________
User ID: ______________ Password: ______________
Notes:

Service: ______________________________
Provider Name: ______________________________
Company Name: ______________________________
Address: ______________________ Unit: __________
City: ______________ State: __________ Zip: __________
Phone Number: ______________________________
Email: ______________________________
Website: ______________________________
User ID: ______________ Password: ______________
Notes:

Service: ______________________________
Provider Name: ______________________________
Company Name: ______________________________
Address: ______________________ Unit: __________
City: ______________ State: __________ Zip: __________
Phone Number: ______________________________
Email: ______________________________
Website: ______________________________
User ID: ______________ Password: ______________
Notes:

HOME LIFE

Service Providers

Service: ______________________________
Provider Name: ______________________________
Company Name: ______________________________
Address: ______________________ Unit: __________
City: ______________ State: ________ Zip: ________
Phone Number: ______________________________
Email: ______________________________
Website: ______________________________
User ID: ______________ Password: ______________
Notes:

Service: ______________________________
Provider Name: ______________________________
Company Name: ______________________________
Address: ______________________ Unit: __________
City: ______________ State: ________ Zip: ________
Phone Number: ______________________________
Email: ______________________________
Website: ______________________________
User ID: ______________ Password: ______________
Notes:

Service: ______________________________
Provider Name: ______________________________
Company Name: ______________________________
Address: ______________________ Unit: __________
City: ______________ State: ________ Zip: ________
Phone Number: ______________________________
Email: ______________________________
Website: ______________________________
User ID: ______________ Password: ______________
Notes:

HOME LIFE
Service Providers

Service: ______
Provider Name: ______
Company Name: ______
Address: ______ Unit: ______
City: ______ State: ______ Zip: ______
Phone Number: ______
Email: ______
Website: ______
User ID: ______ Password: ______
Notes:

Service: ______
Provider Name: ______
Company Name: ______
Address: ______ Unit: ______
City: ______ State: ______ Zip: ______
Phone Number: ______
Email: ______
Website: ______
User ID: ______ Password: ______
Notes:

Service: ______
Provider Name: ______
Company Name: ______
Address: ______ Unit: ______
City: ______ State: ______ Zip: ______
Phone Number: ______
Email: ______
Website: ______
User ID: ______ Password: ______
Notes:

HOME LIFE
Service Providers

Service:
Provider Name:
Company Name:
Address: Unit:
City: State: Zip:
Phone Number:
Email:
Website:
User ID: Password:
Notes:

Service:
Provider Name:
Company Name:
Address: Unit:
City: State: Zip:
Phone Number:
Email:
Website:
User ID: Password:
Notes:

Service:
Provider Name:
Company Name:
Address: Unit:
City: State: Zip:
Phone Number:
Email:
Website:
User ID: Password:
Notes:

HOME LIFE

Service Providers

Service:

Provider Name:

Company Name:

Address: Unit:

City: State: Zip:

Phone Number:

Email:

Website:

User ID: Password:

Notes:

Service:

Provider Name:

Company Name:

Address: Unit:

City: State: Zip:

Phone Number:

Email:

Website:

User ID: Password:

Notes:

Service:

Provider Name:

Company Name:

Address: Unit:

City: State: Zip:

Phone Number:

Email:

Website:

User ID: Password:

Notes:

HOME LIFE
Service Providers

SERVICE:
PROVIDER NAME:
COMPANY NAME:
ADDRESS: UNIT:
CITY: STATE: ZIP:
PHONE NUMBER:
EMAIL:
WEBSITE:
USER ID: PASSWORD:
NOTES:

SERVICE:
PROVIDER NAME:
COMPANY NAME:
ADDRESS: UNIT:
CITY: STATE: ZIP:
PHONE NUMBER:
EMAIL:
WEBSITE:
USER ID: PASSWORD:
NOTES:

SERVICE:
PROVIDER NAME:
COMPANY NAME:
ADDRESS: UNIT:
CITY: STATE: ZIP:
PHONE NUMBER:
EMAIL:
WEBSITE:
USER ID: PASSWORD:
NOTES:

HOME LIFE

Service Providers

Service:
Provider Name:
Company Name:
Address: Unit:
City: State: Zip:
Phone Number:
Email:
Website:
User ID: Password:
Notes:

Service:
Provider Name:
Company Name:
Address: Unit:
City: State: Zip:
Phone Number:
Email:
Website:
User ID: Password:
Notes:

Service:
Provider Name:
Company Name:
Address: Unit:
City: State: Zip:
Phone Number:
Email:
Website:
User ID: Password:
Notes:

HOME LIFE
Service Providers

Service: ______
Provider Name: ______
Company Name: ______
Address: ______ Unit: ______
City: ______ State: ______ Zip: ______
Phone Number: ______
Email: ______
Website: ______
User ID: ______ Password: ______
Notes:

Service: ______
Provider Name: ______
Company Name: ______
Address: ______ Unit: ______
City: ______ State: ______ Zip: ______
Phone Number: ______
Email: ______
Website: ______
User ID: ______ Password: ______
Notes:

Service: ______
Provider Name: ______
Company Name: ______
Address: ______ Unit: ______
City: ______ State: ______ Zip: ______
Phone Number: ______
Email: ______
Website: ______
User ID: ______ Password: ______
Notes:

HOME LIFE

Service Providers

Service: ______________________

Provider Name: ______________________

Company Name: ______________________

Address: ______________ Unit: ______

City: ______________ State: ______ Zip: ______

Phone Number: ______________________

Email: ______________________

Website: ______________________

User ID: ______________ Password: ______________

Notes:

Service: ______________________

Provider Name: ______________________

Company Name: ______________________

Address: ______________ Unit: ______

City: ______________ State: ______ Zip: ______

Phone Number: ______________________

Email: ______________________

Website: ______________________

User ID: ______________ Password: ______________

Notes:

Service: ______________________

Provider Name: ______________________

Company Name: ______________________

Address: ______________ Unit: ______

City: ______________ State: ______ Zip: ______

Phone Number: ______________________

Email: ______________________

Website: ______________________

User ID: ______________ Password: ______________

Notes:

HOME LIFE

Service Providers

Service: ____________________

Provider Name: ____________________

Company Name: ____________________

Address: __________ Unit: ______

City: __________ State: ______ Zip: ______

Phone Number: ____________________

Email: ____________________

Website: ____________________

User ID: __________ Password: __________

Notes:

Service: ____________________

Provider Name: ____________________

Company Name: ____________________

Address: __________ Unit: ______

City: __________ State: ______ Zip: ______

Phone Number: ____________________

Email: ____________________

Website: ____________________

User ID: __________ Password: __________

Notes:

Service: ____________________

Provider Name: ____________________

Company Name: ____________________

Address: __________ Unit: ______

City: __________ State: ______ Zip: ______

Phone Number: ____________________

Email: ____________________

Website: ____________________

User ID: __________ Password: __________

Notes:

HOME LIFE

Service Providers

Service:
Provider Name:
Company Name:
Address: Unit:
City: State: Zip:
Phone Number:
Email:
Website:
User ID: Password:
Notes:

Service:
Provider Name:
Company Name:
Address: Unit:
City: State: Zip:
Phone Number:
Email:
Website:
User ID: Password:
Notes:

Service:
Provider Name:
Company Name:
Address: Unit:
City: State: Zip:
Phone Number:
Email:
Website:
User ID: Password:
Notes:

HOME LIFE

Service Providers

Service: ____________________

Provider Name: ____________________

Company Name: ____________________

Address: ____________________ Unit: __________

City: __________ State: __________ Zip: __________

Phone Number: ____________________

Email: ____________________

Website: ____________________

User ID: __________ Password: __________

Notes:

Service: ____________________

Provider Name: ____________________

Company Name: ____________________

Address: ____________________ Unit: __________

City: __________ State: __________ Zip: __________

Phone Number: ____________________

Email: ____________________

Website: ____________________

User ID: __________ Password: __________

Notes:

Service: ____________________

Provider Name: ____________________

Company Name: ____________________

Address: ____________________ Unit: __________

City: __________ State: __________ Zip: __________

Phone Number: ____________________

Email: ____________________

Website: ____________________

User ID: __________ Password: __________

Notes:

HOME LIFE

Service Providers

Service:
Provider Name:
Company Name:
Address: Unit:
City: State: Zip:
Phone Number:
Email:
Website:
User ID: Password:
Notes:

Service:
Provider Name:
Company Name:
Address: Unit:
City: State: Zip:
Phone Number:
Email:
Website:
User ID: Password:
Notes:

Service:
Provider Name:
Company Name:
Address: Unit:
City: State: Zip:
Phone Number:
Email:
Website:
User ID: Password:
Notes:

HOME LIFE
Service Providers

Service: ______________________________
Provider Name: ______________________________
Company Name: ______________________________
Address: ______________________ Unit: __________
City: ______________ State: __________ Zip: __________
Phone Number: ______________________________
Email: ______________________________
Website: ______________________________
User ID: ______________ Password: ______________
Notes:

Service: ______________________________
Provider Name: ______________________________
Company Name: ______________________________
Address: ______________________ Unit: __________
City: ______________ State: __________ Zip: __________
Phone Number: ______________________________
Email: ______________________________
Website: ______________________________
User ID: ______________ Password: ______________
Notes:

Service: ______________________________
Provider Name: ______________________________
Company Name: ______________________________
Address: ______________________ Unit: __________
City: ______________ State: __________ Zip: __________
Phone Number: ______________________________
Email: ______________________________
Website: ______________________________
User ID: ______________ Password: ______________
Notes:

HOME LIFE

Service Providers

Service:
Provider Name:
Company Name:
Address: Unit:
City: State: Zip:
Phone Number:
Email:
Website:
User ID: Password:
Notes:

Service:
Provider Name:
Company Name:
Address: Unit:
City: State: Zip:
Phone Number:
Email:
Website:
User ID: Password:
Notes:

Service:
Provider Name:
Company Name:
Address: Unit:
City: State: Zip:
Phone Number:
Email:
Website:
User ID: Password:
Notes:

WORK LIFE SECTION

Places I've Worked
Great for resumes and application, keep track of all of your past employers, references, and employment information.

Organizations
Keep track of professional memberships, organizations, roles, and key contacts.

Network
Organize all of your references and business contacts in one place for easy recall.

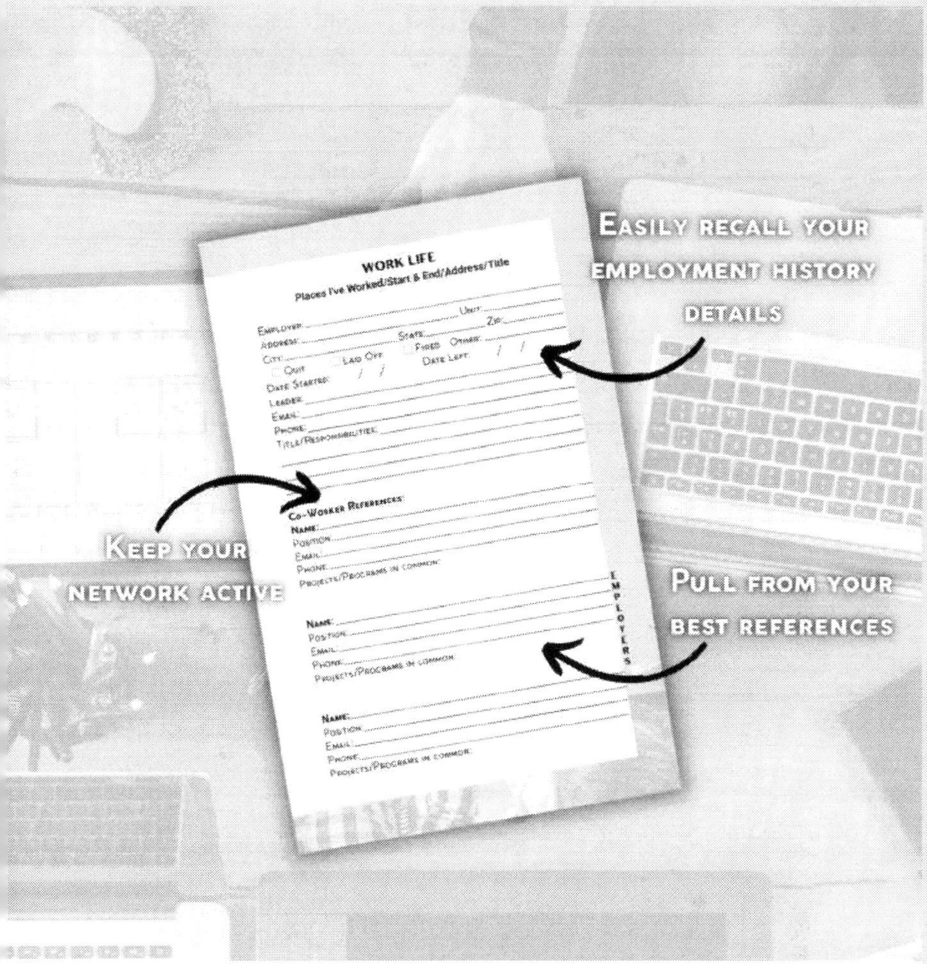

WORK LIFE

Places I've Worked
Organizations
Network

WORK LIFE

Places I've Worked/Start & End/Address/Title

Employer:____
Address: __________________________ Unit:____________
City:____________________ State:__________ Zip:__________
☐ Quit ☐ Laid Off ☐ Fired Other: ______________
Date Started: / / Date Left: / /
Leader: ____
Email: ____
Phone: ____
Title/Responsibilities: ______________________________

Co-Worker References:

Name:____
Position:____
Email:____
Phone:____
Projects/Programs in common:

Name:____
Position:____
Email:____
Phone:____
Projects/Programs in common:

Name:____
Position:____
Email:____
Phone:____
Projects/Programs in common:

WORK LIFE
Professional Organizations

Organization: ______________________________
Address: ______________________ Unit: ________
City: ______________ State: __________ Zip: ________
Date Joined: / /
Website: ______________________________
User ID: ______________ Password: ______________
Associated Email: ______________________________
Email: ______________________________
Phone: ______________________________
Dues: ______________ Owed: Annually ☐ Monthly ☐
Annual Conference: ______________________________
Meeting Times: ______________________________
Title/Responsibilities:

Network:
Name: ______________________________
Position: ______________________________
Email: ______________________________
Phone: ______________________________
Projects/Programs in common:

Name: ______________________________
Position: ______________________________
Email: ______________________________
Phone: ______________________________
Projects/Programs in common:

Name: ______________________________
Position: ______________________________
Email: ______________________________
Phone: ______________________________
Projects/Programs in common:

WORK LIFE
Professional Organizations

ORGANIZATION: ____________________
ADDRESS: ____________________ UNIT: __________
CITY: __________ STATE: __________ ZIP: __________
DATE JOINED: / /
WEBSITE: ____________________
USER ID: __________ PASSWORD: __________
ASSOCIATED EMAIL: ____________________
EMAIL: ____________________
PHONE: ____________________
DUES: __________ OWED: ANNUALLY ☐ MONTHLY ☐
ANNUAL CONFERENCE: ____________________
MEETING TIMES: ____________________
TITLE/RESPONSIBILITIES:

NETWORK:
NAME: ____________________
POSITION: ____________________
EMAIL: ____________________
PHONE: ____________________
PROJECTS/PROGRAMS IN COMMON:

NAME: ____________________
POSITION: ____________________
EMAIL: ____________________
PHONE: ____________________
PROJECTS/PROGRAMS IN COMMON:

NAME: ____________________
POSITION: ____________________
EMAIL: ____________________
PHONE: ____________________
PROJECTS/PROGRAMS IN COMMON:

WORK LIFE

Professional Organizations

Organization: ____________________
Address: ____________________ Unit: __________
City: __________ State: __________ Zip: __________
Date Joined: / /
Website: ____________________
User ID: __________ Password: __________
Associated Email: ____________________
Email: ____________________
Phone: ____________________
Dues: __________ Owed: Annually ☐ Monthly ☐
Annual Conference: ____________________
Meeting Times: ____________________
Title/Responsibilities:

Network:
Name: ____________________
Position: ____________________
Email: ____________________
Phone: ____________________
Projects/Programs in common:

Name: ____________________
Position: ____________________
Email: ____________________
Phone: ____________________
Projects/Programs in common:

Name: ____________________
Position: ____________________
Email: ____________________
Phone: ____________________
Projects/Programs in common:

WORK LIFE

Professional Organizations

Organization: ______________________________

Address: ______________________ Unit: __________

City: ______________ State: __________ Zip: __________

Date Joined: / /

Website: ______________________________

User ID: ______________ Password: ______________

Associated Email: ______________________________

Email: ______________________________

Phone: ______________________________

Dues: ______________ Owed: Annually ☐ Monthly ☐

Annual Conference: ______________________________

Meeting Times: ______________________________

Title/Responsibilities:

Network:

Name: ______________________________

Position: ______________________________

Email: ______________________________

Phone: ______________________________

Projects/Programs in common:

Name: ______________________________

Position: ______________________________

Email: ______________________________

Phone: ______________________________

Projects/Programs in common:

Name: ______________________________

Position: ______________________________

Email: ______________________________

Phone: ______________________________

Projects/Programs in common:

WORK LIFE
Professional Organizations

Organization: ______________________________
Address: ______________________ Unit: __________
City: ______________ State: __________ Zip: __________
Date Joined: / /
Website: ______________________________
User ID: ______________ Password: ______________
Associated Email: ______________________________
Email: ______________________________
Phone: ______________________________
Dues: ______________ Owed: Annually ☐ Monthly ☐
Annual Conference: ______________________________
Meeting Times: ______________________________
Title/Responsibilities:

Network:
Name: ______________________________
Position: ______________________________
Email: ______________________________
Phone: ______________________________
Projects/Programs in common:

Name: ______________________________
Position: ______________________________
Email: ______________________________
Phone: ______________________________
Projects/Programs in common:

Name: ______________________________
Position: ______________________________
Email: ______________________________
Phone: ______________________________
Projects/Programs in common:

WORK LIFE

Professional Organizations

Organization: ______________________________

Address: ______________________ Unit: __________

City: ______________ State: __________ Zip: __________

Date Joined: / /

Website: ______________________________

User ID: ______________ Password: ______________

Associated Email: ______________________________

Email: ______________________________

Phone: ______________________________

Dues: ______________ Owed: Annually ☐ Monthly ☐

Annual Conference: ______________________________

Meeting Times: ______________________________

Title/Responsibilities:

Network:

Name: ______________________________

Position: ______________________________

Email: ______________________________

Phone: ______________________________

Projects/Programs in common:

Name: ______________________________

Position: ______________________________

Email: ______________________________

Phone: ______________________________

Projects/Programs in common:

Name: ______________________________

Position: ______________________________

Email: ______________________________

Phone: ______________________________

Projects/Programs in common:

WORK LIFE

Professional Organizations

Organization: ______________________________

Address: ______________________ Unit: __________

City: ______________ State: __________ Zip: __________

Date Joined: / /

Website: ______________________________

User ID: ______________ Password: ______________

Associated Email: ______________________________

Email: ______________________________

Phone: ______________________________

Dues: ______________ Owed: Annually ☐ Monthly ☐

Annual Conference: ______________________________

Meeting Times: ______________________________

Title/Responsibilities:

Network:

Name: ______________________________

Position: ______________________________

Email: ______________________________

Phone: ______________________________

Projects/Programs in common:

Name: ______________________________

Position: ______________________________

Email: ______________________________

Phone: ______________________________

Projects/Programs in common:

Name: ______________________________

Position: ______________________________

Email: ______________________________

Phone: ______________________________

Projects/Programs in common:

WORK LIFE

Professional Organizations

Organization: ____________________
Address: ____________________ Unit: __________
City: __________ State: __________ Zip: __________
Date Joined: / /
Website: ____________________
User ID: __________ Password: __________
Associated Email: ____________________
Email: ____________________
Phone: ____________________
Dues: __________ Owed: Annually ☐ Monthly ☐
Annual Conference: ____________________
Meeting Times: ____________________
Title/Responsibilities:

Network:
Name: ____________________
Position: ____________________
Email: ____________________
Phone: ____________________
Projects/Programs in common:

Name: ____________________
Position: ____________________
Email: ____________________
Phone: ____________________
Projects/Programs in common:

Name: ____________________
Position: ____________________
Email: ____________________
Phone: ____________________
Projects/Programs in common:

WORK LIFE

Professional Organizations

Organization: ______________________________
Address: ____________________ Unit: ________
City: ____________ State: ________ Zip: ________
Date Joined: / /
Website: ______________________________
User ID: ____________ Password: ____________
Associated Email: ________________________
Email: ______________________________
Phone: ______________________________
Dues: ____________ Owed: Annually ☐ Monthly ☐
Annual Conference: ________________________
Meeting Times: __________________________
Title/Responsibilities:

Network:

Name: ______________________________
Position: ______________________________
Email: ______________________________
Phone: ______________________________
Projects/Programs in common:

Name: ______________________________
Position: ______________________________
Email: ______________________________
Phone: ______________________________
Projects/Programs in common:

Name: ______________________________
Position: ______________________________
Email: ______________________________
Phone: ______________________________
Projects/Programs in common:

WORK LIFE
Professional Organizations

ORGANIZATION: ______________________________
ADDRESS: ______________________ UNIT: __________
CITY: ______________ STATE: __________ ZIP: __________
DATE JOINED: / /
WEBSITE: ______________________________
USER ID: ______________ PASSWORD: ______________
ASSOCIATED EMAIL: ______________________________
EMAIL: ______________________________
PHONE: ______________________________
DUES: ______________ OWED: ANNUALLY ☐ MONTHLY ☐
ANNUAL CONFERENCE: ______________________________
MEETING TIMES: ______________________________
TITLE/RESPONSIBILITIES:

NETWORK:
NAME: ______________________________
POSITION: ______________________________
EMAIL: ______________________________
PHONE: ______________________________
PROJECTS/PROGRAMS IN COMMON:

NAME: ______________________________
POSITION: ______________________________
EMAIL: ______________________________
PHONE: ______________________________
PROJECTS/PROGRAMS IN COMMON:

NAME: ______________________________
POSITION: ______________________________
EMAIL: ______________________________
PHONE: ______________________________
PROJECTS/PROGRAMS IN COMMON:

WORK LIFE

Professional Network

Name: ______________________________
Position: ______________________________
Email: ______________________________
Phone: ______________________________
Projects/Programs in common:

Name: ______________________________
Position: ______________________________
Email: ______________________________
Phone: ______________________________
Projects/Programs in common:

Name: ______________________________
Position: ______________________________
Email: ______________________________
Phone: ______________________________
Projects/Programs in common:

Name: ______________________________
Position: ______________________________
Email: ______________________________
Phone: ______________________________
Projects/Programs in common:

Name: ______________________________
Position: ______________________________
Email: ______________________________
Phone: ______________________________
Projects/Programs in common:

Name: ______________________________
Position: ______________________________
Email: ______________________________
Phone: ______________________________
Projects/Programs in common:

WORK LIFE

Professional Network

NAME: ______________________
POSITION: ______________________
EMAIL: ______________________
PHONE: ______________________
PROJECTS/PROGRAMS IN COMMON:

NAME: ______________________
POSITION: ______________________
EMAIL: ______________________
PHONE: ______________________
PROJECTS/PROGRAMS IN COMMON:

NAME: ______________________
POSITION: ______________________
EMAIL: ______________________
PHONE: ______________________
PROJECTS/PROGRAMS IN COMMON:

NAME: ______________________
POSITION: ______________________
EMAIL: ______________________
PHONE: ______________________
PROJECTS/PROGRAMS IN COMMON:

NAME: ______________________
POSITION: ______________________
EMAIL: ______________________
PHONE: ______________________
PROJECTS/PROGRAMS IN COMMON:

NAME: ______________________
POSITION: ______________________
EMAIL: ______________________
PHONE: ______________________
PROJECTS/PROGRAMS IN COMMON:

WORK LIFE

Professional Network

NAME: ____________________
POSITION: ____________________
EMAIL: ____________________
PHONE: ____________________
PROJECTS/PROGRAMS IN COMMON:

NAME: ____________________
POSITION: ____________________
EMAIL: ____________________
PHONE: ____________________
PROJECTS/PROGRAMS IN COMMON:

NAME: ____________________
POSITION: ____________________
EMAIL: ____________________
PHONE: ____________________
PROJECTS/PROGRAMS IN COMMON:

NAME: ____________________
POSITION: ____________________
EMAIL: ____________________
PHONE: ____________________
PROJECTS/PROGRAMS IN COMMON:

NAME: ____________________
POSITION: ____________________
EMAIL: ____________________
PHONE: ____________________
PROJECTS/PROGRAMS IN COMMON:

NAME: ____________________
POSITION: ____________________
EMAIL: ____________________
PHONE: ____________________
PROJECTS/PROGRAMS IN COMMON:

WORK LIFE

Professional Network

NAME: ____________________
POSITION: ____________________
EMAIL: ____________________
PHONE: ____________________
PROJECTS/PROGRAMS IN COMMON:

NAME: ____________________
POSITION: ____________________
EMAIL: ____________________
PHONE: ____________________
PROJECTS/PROGRAMS IN COMMON:

NAME: ____________________
POSITION: ____________________
EMAIL: ____________________
PHONE: ____________________
PROJECTS/PROGRAMS IN COMMON:

NAME: ____________________
POSITION: ____________________
EMAIL: ____________________
PHONE: ____________________
PROJECTS/PROGRAMS IN COMMON:

NAME: ____________________
POSITION: ____________________
EMAIL: ____________________
PHONE: ____________________
PROJECTS/PROGRAMS IN COMMON:

NAME: ____________________
POSITION: ____________________
EMAIL: ____________________
PHONE: ____________________
PROJECTS/PROGRAMS IN COMMON:

WORK LIFE

Professional Network

Name: ____________________
Position: ____________________
Email: ____________________
Phone: ____________________
Projects/Programs in common:

Name: ____________________
Position: ____________________
Email: ____________________
Phone: ____________________
Projects/Programs in common:

Name: ____________________
Position: ____________________
Email: ____________________
Phone: ____________________
Projects/Programs in common:

Name: ____________________
Position: ____________________
Email: ____________________
Phone: ____________________
Projects/Programs in common:

Name: ____________________
Position: ____________________
Email: ____________________
Phone: ____________________
Projects/Programs in common:

Name: ____________________
Position: ____________________
Email: ____________________
Phone: ____________________
Projects/Programs in common:

WORK LIFE

Professional Network

NAME:
POSITION:
EMAIL:
PHONE:
PROJECTS/PROGRAMS IN COMMON:

NAME:
POSITION:
EMAIL:
PHONE:
PROJECTS/PROGRAMS IN COMMON:

NAME:
POSITION:
EMAIL:
PHONE:
PROJECTS/PROGRAMS IN COMMON:

NAME:
POSITION:
EMAIL:
PHONE:
PROJECTS/PROGRAMS IN COMMON:

NAME:
POSITION:
EMAIL:
PHONE:
PROJECTS/PROGRAMS IN COMMON:

NAME:
POSITION:
EMAIL:
PHONE:
PROJECTS/PROGRAMS IN COMMON:

WORK LIFE

Professional Network

Name: ____________________
Position: ____________________
Email: ____________________
Phone: ____________________
Projects/Programs in common:

Name: ____________________
Position: ____________________
Email: ____________________
Phone: ____________________
Projects/Programs in common:

Name: ____________________
Position: ____________________
Email: ____________________
Phone: ____________________
Projects/Programs in common:

Name: ____________________
Position: ____________________
Email: ____________________
Phone: ____________________
Projects/Programs in common:

Name: ____________________
Position: ____________________
Email: ____________________
Phone: ____________________
Projects/Programs in common:

Name: ____________________
Position: ____________________
Email: ____________________
Phone: ____________________
Projects/Programs in common:

WORK LIFE

Professional Network

NAME: ______
POSITION: ______
EMAIL: ______
PHONE: ______
PROJECTS/PROGRAMS IN COMMON:

NAME: ______
POSITION: ______
EMAIL: ______
PHONE: ______
PROJECTS/PROGRAMS IN COMMON:

NAME: ______
POSITION: ______
EMAIL: ______
PHONE: ______
PROJECTS/PROGRAMS IN COMMON:

NAME: ______
POSITION: ______
EMAIL: ______
PHONE: ______
PROJECTS/PROGRAMS IN COMMON:

NETWORK

NAME: ______
POSITION: ______
EMAIL: ______
PHONE: ______
PROJECTS/PROGRAMS IN COMMON:

NAME: ______
POSITION: ______
EMAIL: ______
PHONE: ______
PROJECTS/PROGRAMS IN COMMON:

WORK LIFE

Professional Network

NAME: ______________________________
POSITION: ______________________________
EMAIL: ______________________________
PHONE: ______________________________
PROJECTS/PROGRAMS IN COMMON:

NAME: ______________________________
POSITION: ______________________________
EMAIL: ______________________________
PHONE: ______________________________
PROJECTS/PROGRAMS IN COMMON:

NAME: ______________________________
POSITION: ______________________________
EMAIL: ______________________________
PHONE: ______________________________
PROJECTS/PROGRAMS IN COMMON:

NAME: ______________________________
POSITION: ______________________________
EMAIL: ______________________________
PHONE: ______________________________
PROJECTS/PROGRAMS IN COMMON:

NAME: ______________________________
POSITION: ______________________________
EMAIL: ______________________________
PHONE: ______________________________
PROJECTS/PROGRAMS IN COMMON:

NAME: ______________________________
POSITION: ______________________________
EMAIL: ______________________________
PHONE: ______________________________
PROJECTS/PROGRAMS IN COMMON:

WORK LIFE

Professional Network

NAME: ____________________
POSITION: ____________________
EMAIL: ____________________
PHONE: ____________________
PROJECTS/PROGRAMS IN COMMON:

NAME: ____________________
POSITION: ____________________
EMAIL: ____________________
PHONE: ____________________
PROJECTS/PROGRAMS IN COMMON:

NAME: ____________________
POSITION: ____________________
EMAIL: ____________________
PHONE: ____________________
PROJECTS/PROGRAMS IN COMMON:

NAME: ____________________
POSITION: ____________________
EMAIL: ____________________
PHONE: ____________________
PROJECTS/PROGRAMS IN COMMON:

NAME: ____________________
POSITION: ____________________
EMAIL: ____________________
PHONE: ____________________
PROJECTS/PROGRAMS IN COMMON:

NAME: ____________________
POSITION: ____________________
EMAIL: ____________________
PHONE: ____________________
PROJECTS/PROGRAMS IN COMMON:

WORK LIFE

Professional Network

NAME: ____________________
POSITION: ____________________
EMAIL: ____________________
PHONE: ____________________
PROJECTS/PROGRAMS IN COMMON:

NAME: ____________________
POSITION: ____________________
EMAIL: ____________________
PHONE: ____________________
PROJECTS/PROGRAMS IN COMMON:

NAME: ____________________
POSITION: ____________________
EMAIL: ____________________
PHONE: ____________________
PROJECTS/PROGRAMS IN COMMON:

NAME: ____________________
POSITION: ____________________
EMAIL: ____________________
PHONE: ____________________
PROJECTS/PROGRAMS IN COMMON:

NAME: ____________________
POSITION: ____________________
EMAIL: ____________________
PHONE: ____________________
PROJECTS/PROGRAMS IN COMMON:

NAME: ____________________
POSITION: ____________________
EMAIL: ____________________
PHONE: ____________________
PROJECTS/PROGRAMS IN COMMON:

SOCIAL LIFE SECTION

Friends/References/Acquaintances
Keep Track of important details on your social network like birthdays, family members, and important information.

Social Clubs/Charities

SOCIAL LIFE

Friends/References/Acquaintances
Social Clubs/Charities

SOCIAL LIFE

Friends/References/Acquaintances

SOCIAL CIRCLE/GROUP: ____________________

FRIENDS ☐ **CLOSE** ☐ **ACQUAINTANCE** ☐ **CAN BE REFERENCE** ☐

NAME: ____________________ BIRTHDAY: __________

SPOUSE: ____________________ BIRTHDAY: __________

CHILDREN: ____________________ BIRTHDAY: __________

BIRTHDAY: __________

ADDRESS: ____________________

PHONE NUMBER: ____________________

EMAIL: ____________________

HOW MET/NOTES:

SOCIAL CIRCLE/GROUP: ____________________

FRIENDS ☐ **CLOSE** ☐ **ACQUAINTANCE** ☐ **CAN BE REFERENCE** ☐

NAME: ____________________ BIRTHDAY: __________

SPOUSE: ____________________ BIRTHDAY: __________

CHILDREN: ____________________ BIRTHDAY: __________

BIRTHDAY: __________

ADDRESS: ____________________

PHONE NUMBER: ____________________

EMAIL: ____________________

HOW MET/NOTES:

SOCIAL CIRCLE/GROUP: ____________________

FRIENDS ☐ **CLOSE** ☐ **ACQUAINTANCE** ☐ **CAN BE REFERENCE** ☐

NAME: ____________________ BIRTHDAY: __________

SPOUSE: ____________________ BIRTHDAY: __________

CHILDREN: ____________________ BIRTHDAY: __________

BIRTHDAY: __________

ADDRESS: ____________________

PHONE NUMBER: ____________________

EMAIL: ____________________

HOW MET/NOTES:

SOCIAL LIFE

Friends/References/Acquaintances

Social Circle/Group: ____________________

Friends ☐ **Close** ☐ **Acquaintance** ☐ **Can be Reference** ☐

Name: ____________________ Birthday: __________

Spouse: ____________________ Birthday: __________

Children: ____________________ Birthday: __________

____________________ Birthday: __________

Address: ____________________

____

Phone Number: ____________________

Email: ____________________

How Met/Notes:

Social Circle/Group: ____________________

Friends ☐ **Close** ☐ **Acquaintance** ☐ **Can be Reference** ☐

Name: ____________________ Birthday: __________

Spouse: ____________________ Birthday: __________

Children: ____________________ Birthday: __________

____________________ Birthday: __________

Address: ____________________

____

Phone Number: ____________________

Email: ____________________

How Met/Notes:

Social Circle/Group: ____________________

Friends ☐ **Close** ☐ **Acquaintance** ☐ **Can be Reference** ☐

Name: ____________________ Birthday: __________

Spouse: ____________________ Birthday: __________

Children: ____________________ Birthday: __________

____________________ Birthday: __________

Address: ____________________

____

Phone Number: ____________________

Email: ____________________

How Met/Notes:

SOCIAL LIFE

Friends/References/Acquaintances

Social Circle/Group: ______

Friends ☐ **Close** ☐ **Acquaintance** ☐ **Can be Reference** ☐

Name: ______ Birthday: ______

Spouse: ______ Birthday: ______

Children: ______ Birthday: ______

Birthday: ______

Address: ______

______

Phone Number: ______

Email: ______

How Met/Notes:

Social Circle/Group: ______

Friends ☐ **Close** ☐ **Acquaintance** ☐ **Can be Reference** ☐

Name: ______ Birthday: ______

Spouse: ______ Birthday: ______

Children: ______ Birthday: ______

Birthday: ______

Address: ______

______

Phone Number: ______

Email: ______

How Met/Notes:

Social Circle/Group: ______

Friends ☐ **Close** ☐ **Acquaintance** ☐ **Can be Reference** ☐

Name: ______ Birthday: ______

Spouse: ______ Birthday: ______

Children: ______ Birthday: ______

Birthday: ______

Address: ______

______

Phone Number: ______

Email: ______

How Met/Notes:

SOCIAL LIFE

Friends/References/Acquaintances

Social Circle/Group: ____________________

Friends ☐ **Close** ☐ **Acquaintance** ☐ **Can be Reference** ☐

Name: ____________________ Birthday: __________

Spouse: ____________________ Birthday: __________

Children: ____________________ Birthday: __________

____________________ Birthday: __________

Address: ____________________

____

Phone Number: ____________________

Email: ____________________

How Met/Notes:

Social Circle/Group: ____________________

Friends ☐ **Close** ☐ **Acquaintance** ☐ **Can be Reference** ☐

Name: ____________________ Birthday: __________

Spouse: ____________________ Birthday: __________

Children: ____________________ Birthday: __________

____________________ Birthday: __________

Address: ____________________

____

Phone Number: ____________________

Email: ____________________

How Met/Notes:

Social Circle/Group: ____________________

Friends ☐ **Close** ☐ **Acquaintance** ☐ **Can be Reference** ☐

Name: ____________________ Birthday: __________

Spouse: ____________________ Birthday: __________

Children: ____________________ Birthday: __________

____________________ Birthday: __________

Address: ____________________

____

Phone Number: ____________________

Email: ____________________

How Met/Notes:

SOCIAL LIFE

Friends/References/Acquaintances

Social Circle/Group: ______

Friends ☐ **Close** ☐ **Acquaintance** ☐ **Can be Reference** ☐

Name: ______ Birthday: ______

Spouse: ______ Birthday: ______

Children: ______ Birthday: ______

Birthday: ______

Address: ______

______

Phone Number: ______

Email: ______

How Met/Notes:

Social Circle/Group: ______

Friends ☐ **Close** ☐ **Acquaintance** ☐ **Can be Reference** ☐

Name: ______ Birthday: ______

Spouse: ______ Birthday: ______

Children: ______ Birthday: ______

Birthday: ______

Address: ______

______

Phone Number: ______

Email: ______

How Met/Notes:

Social Circle/Group: ______

Friends ☐ **Close** ☐ **Acquaintance** ☐ **Can be Reference** ☐

Name: ______ Birthday: ______

Spouse: ______ Birthday: ______

Children: ______ Birthday: ______

Birthday: ______

Address: ______

______

Phone Number: ______

Email: ______

How Met/Notes:

SOCIAL LIFE

Friends/References/Acquaintances

Social Circle/Group: ____________

Friends ☐ **Close** ☐ **Acquaintance** ☐ **Can be Reference** ☐

Name: ____________ Birthday: ____________

Spouse: ____________ Birthday: ____________

Children: ____________ Birthday: ____________

____________ Birthday: ____________

Address: ____________

____

Phone Number: ____________

Email: ____________

How Met/Notes:

Social Circle/Group: ____________

Friends ☐ **Close** ☐ **Acquaintance** ☐ **Can be Reference** ☐

Name: ____________ Birthday: ____________

Spouse: ____________ Birthday: ____________

Children: ____________ Birthday: ____________

____________ Birthday: ____________

Address: ____________

____

Phone Number: ____________

Email: ____________

How Met/Notes:

Social Circle/Group: ____________

Friends ☐ **Close** ☐ **Acquaintance** ☐ **Can be Reference** ☐

Name: ____________ Birthday: ____________

Spouse: ____________ Birthday: ____________

Children: ____________ Birthday: ____________

____________ Birthday: ____________

Address: ____________

____

Phone Number: ____________

Email: ____________

How Met/Notes:

SOCIAL LIFE

Friends/References/Acquaintances

SOCIAL CIRCLE/GROUP: ____________________

FRIENDS ☐ **CLOSE** ☐ **ACQUAINTANCE** ☐ **CAN BE REFERENCE** ☐

NAME: ____________________ BIRTHDAY: __________

SPOUSE: ____________________ BIRTHDAY: __________

CHILDREN: ____________________ BIRTHDAY: __________

____________________ BIRTHDAY: __________

ADDRESS: ____________________

____

PHONE NUMBER: ____________________

EMAIL: ____________________

HOW MET/NOTES:

SOCIAL CIRCLE/GROUP: ____________________

FRIENDS ☐ **CLOSE** ☐ **ACQUAINTANCE** ☐ **CAN BE REFERENCE** ☐

NAME: ____________________ BIRTHDAY: __________

SPOUSE: ____________________ BIRTHDAY: __________

CHILDREN: ____________________ BIRTHDAY: __________

____________________ BIRTHDAY: __________

ADDRESS: ____________________

____

PHONE NUMBER: ____________________

EMAIL: ____________________

HOW MET/NOTES:

SOCIAL CIRCLE/GROUP: ____________________

FRIENDS ☐ **CLOSE** ☐ **ACQUAINTANCE** ☐ **CAN BE REFERENCE** ☐

NAME: ____________________ BIRTHDAY: __________

SPOUSE: ____________________ BIRTHDAY: __________

CHILDREN: ____________________ BIRTHDAY: __________

____________________ BIRTHDAY: __________

ADDRESS: ____________________

____

PHONE NUMBER: ____________________

EMAIL: ____________________

HOW MET/NOTES:

SOCIAL LIFE

Friends/References/Acquaintances

Social Circle/Group: ______

Friends ☐ **Close** ☐ **Acquaintance** ☐ **Can be Reference** ☐

Name: ______ Birthday: ______

Spouse: ______ Birthday: ______

Children: ______ Birthday: ______

______ Birthday: ______

Address: ______

______

Phone Number: ______

Email: ______

How Met/Notes:

Social Circle/Group: ______

Friends ☐ **Close** ☐ **Acquaintance** ☐ **Can be Reference** ☐

Name: ______ Birthday: ______

Spouse: ______ Birthday: ______

Children: ______ Birthday: ______

______ Birthday: ______

Address: ______

______

Phone Number: ______

Email: ______

How Met/Notes:

Social Circle/Group: ______

Friends ☐ **Close** ☐ **Acquaintance** ☐ **Can be Reference** ☐

Name: ______ Birthday: ______

Spouse: ______ Birthday: ______

Children: ______ Birthday: ______

______ Birthday: ______

Address: ______

______

Phone Number: ______

Email: ______

How Met/Notes:

SOCIAL LIFE
Social Clubs/Charities

Organization: ____________________

Address: ____________________ Unit: __________

City: __________ State: __________ Zip: __________

Date Joined: / /

Website: ____________________

User ID: __________ Password: __________

Associated Email: ____________________

Email: ____________________

Phone: ____________________

Dues: __________ Owed: Annually ☐ Monthly ☐

Annual Conference: ____________________

Meeting Times: ____________________

Title/Responsibilities:

Network:

Name: ____________________

Position: ____________________

Email: ____________________

Phone: ____________________

Projects/Programs in common:

Name: ____________________

Position: ____________________

Email: ____________________

Phone: ____________________

Projects/Programs in common:

Name: ____________________

Position: ____________________

Email: ____________________

Phone: ____________________

Projects/Programs in common:

SOCIAL LIFE

Social Clubs/Charities

Organization: ____________________

Address: ____________________ Unit: __________

City: ______________ State: __________ Zip: __________

Date Joined: / /

Website: ____________________

User ID: ______________ Password: ______________

Associated Email: ____________________

Email: ____________________

Phone: ____________________

Dues: ______________ Owed: Annually ☐ Monthly ☐

Annual Conference: ____________________

Meeting Times: ____________________

Title/Responsibilities:

Network:

Name: ____________________

Position: ____________________

Email: ____________________

Phone: ____________________

Projects/Programs in common:

Name: ____________________

Position: ____________________

Email: ____________________

Phone: ____________________

Projects/Programs in common:

Name: ____________________

Position: ____________________

Email: ____________________

Phone: ____________________

Projects/Programs in common:

SOCIAL LIFE

Social Clubs/Charities

Organization: ______________________________

Address: ______________________ Unit: __________

City: ______________ State: __________ Zip: __________

Date Joined: / /

Website: ______________________________

User ID: ______________ Password: ______________

Associated Email: ______________________________

Email: ______________________________

Phone: ______________________________

Dues: ______________ Owed: Annually ☐ Monthly ☐

Annual Conference: ______________________________

Meeting Times: ______________________________

Title/Responsibilities:

Network:

Name: ______________________________

Position: ______________________________

Email: ______________________________

Phone: ______________________________

Projects/Programs in common:

Name: ______________________________

Position: ______________________________

Email: ______________________________

Phone: ______________________________

Projects/Programs in common:

Name: ______________________________

Position: ______________________________

Email: ______________________________

Phone: ______________________________

Projects/Programs in common:

SOCIAL LIFE
Social Clubs/Charities

Organization: ______________________

Address: ______________________ Unit: __________

City: ______________ State: __________ Zip: __________

Date Joined: / /

Website: ______________________

User ID: ______________ Password: ______________

Associated Email: ______________________

Email: ______________________

Phone: ______________________

Dues: ______________ Owed: Annually ☐ Monthly ☐

Annual Conference: ______________________

Meeting Times: ______________________

Title/Responsibilities:

Network:

Name: ______________________

Position: ______________________

Email: ______________________

Phone: ______________________

Projects/Programs in common:

Name: ______________________

Position: ______________________

Email: ______________________

Phone: ______________________

Projects/Programs in common:

Name: ______________________

Position: ______________________

Email: ______________________

Phone: ______________________

Projects/Programs in common:

SOCIAL LIFE
Social Clubs/Charities

Organization: ____________________
Address: ____________________ Unit: __________
City: __________ State: __________ Zip: __________
Date Joined: / /
Website: ____________________
User ID: __________ Password: __________
Associated Email: ____________________
Email: ____________________
Phone: ____________________
Dues: __________ Owed: Annually ☐ Monthly ☐
Annual Conference: ____________________
Meeting Times: ____________________
Title/Responsibilities:

Network:
Name: ____________________
Position: ____________________
Email: ____________________
Phone: ____________________
Projects/Programs in common:

Name: ____________________
Position: ____________________
Email: ____________________
Phone: ____________________
Projects/Programs in common:

Name: ____________________
Position: ____________________
Email: ____________________
Phone: ____________________
Projects/Programs in common:

SOCIAL LIFE

Social Clubs/Charities

Organization: ____________________

Address: ____________________ Unit: __________

City: __________ State: __________ Zip: __________

Date Joined: / /

Website: ____________________

User ID: __________ Password: __________

Associated Email: ____________________

Email: ____________________

Phone: ____________________

Dues: __________ Owed: Annually ☐ Monthly ☐

Annual Conference: ____________________

Meeting Times: ____________________

Title/Responsibilities:

Network:

Name: ____________________

Position: ____________________

Email: ____________________

Phone: ____________________

Projects/Programs in common:

Name: ____________________

Position: ____________________

Email: ____________________

Phone: ____________________

Projects/Programs in common:

Name: ____________________

Position: ____________________

Email: ____________________

Phone: ____________________

Projects/Programs in common:

SOCIAL LIFE
Social Clubs/Charities

Organization: ______________________________
Address: ______________________ Unit: __________
City: ______________ State: __________ Zip: __________
Date Joined: / /
Website: ______________________________
User ID: ______________ Password: ______________
Associated Email: ______________________________
Email: ______________________________
Phone: ______________________________
Dues: ______________ Owed: Annually ☐ Monthly ☐
Annual Conference: ______________________________
Meeting Times: ______________________________
Title/Responsibilities:

Network:
Name: ______________________________
Position: ______________________________
Email: ______________________________
Phone: ______________________________
Projects/Programs in common:

Name: ______________________________
Position: ______________________________
Email: ______________________________
Phone: ______________________________
Projects/Programs in common:

Name: ______________________________
Position: ______________________________
Email: ______________________________
Phone: ______________________________
Projects/Programs in common:

SOCIAL LIFE

Social Clubs/Charities

Organization: ______________________________

Address: ______________________ Unit: __________

City: ______________ State: __________ Zip: __________

Date Joined: / /

Website: ______________________________

User ID: ______________ Password: ______________

Associated Email: ______________________________

Email: ______________________________

Phone: ______________________________

Dues: ______________ Owed: Annually ☐ Monthly ☐

Annual Conference: ______________________________

Meeting Times: ______________________________

Title/Responsibilities:

Network:

Name: ______________________________

Position: ______________________________

Email: ______________________________

Phone: ______________________________

Projects/Programs in common:

Name: ______________________________

Position: ______________________________

Email: ______________________________

Phone: ______________________________

Projects/Programs in common:

Name: ______________________________

Position: ______________________________

Email: ______________________________

Phone: ______________________________

Projects/Programs in common:

NOTES/MISC.

NOTES/MISC.

NOTES/MISC.

NOTES/MISC.

NOTES/MISC.

NOTES/MISC.

NOTES/MISC.

NOTES/MISC.

NOTES/MISC.

NOTES/MISC.

NOTES/MISC.

NOTES/MISC.

NOTES/MISC.

NOTES/MISC.

NOTES/MISC.

NOTES/MISC.

Made in the USA
Monee, IL
12 November 2026

eb6bfc06-cbc5-4c3e-8820-cb706ba9678cR01